The Dancing Steward

Exploring Christian Stewardship Lifestyles

The Dancing Steward

Exploring Christian Stewardship Lifestyles

Christopher Levan

THE UNITED CHURCH PUBLISHING HOUSE

Canadian Cataloguing in Publication Data

Levan, Christopher, 1953–
 The dancing steward : exploring Christian
stewardship lifestyles

Includes bibliographical references.
ISBN 1-55134-004-6

1. Stewardship, Christian. I. Title.

BV772.L48 1993 248'.6 C93-094519-0

The United Church Publishing House
85 St. Clair Avenue East
Toronto, Ontario
M4T 1M8

Publisher: R.L. Naylor
Editor-in-Chief: Peter Gordon White
Project Editor: Elizabeth Phinney
Book Design: Department of Graphics and Print
Cover Photo: COMSTOCK/Comstock
Printed in Canada by: Kromar Printing Ltd.

5 4 3 2 1 93 94 95 96 97

To Douglas John Hall,
my good friend and wise teacher.

Contents

Acknowledgements

A popular folk song contains the lines, "No one is an island. No one stands alone." There is no situation where this is more true than in the composition of a book. That is my experience at any rate. While the long hours of thinking and typing are carried out in isolation, the inspiration and ideas are the result of a communal effort. Friends, family, colleagues, students, and parishioners have all contributed.

I would like to thank those people who wittingly or unwittingly collaborated in the preliminary stages of this work. Many of the ideas have been presented and tested elsewhere, particularly at stewardship conferences sponsored by the Ecumenical Centre for Stewardship Studies. I would therefore like to thank the executive director of that organization, Ron Vallet, for his understanding and encouragement. Ron has a willing ear for new ideas about stewardship and a kind but critical mind to help sort the wheat from the chaff. It was through Ron that this material was first presented to a meeting of the stewardship personnel from the American Baptist Churches in Clearwater, Florida, in February 1990.

I also owe a debt of gratitude to my friends and fellow travellers in the Department of Stewardship Services of The United Church of Canada. They are a very special group of people: serious about stewardship, fun loving, and kind. Vince Alfano, the director of that department, has been a constant source of encouragement and support. He has always been eager to guide me through the strange cities in which we met.

The insights and advice from students and colleagues at McGill University's Faculty of Religious Studies and at Queen's Theological College are never far from my mind as I work in this field. I think especially of Dan Fraikin, Bill Morrow, Brian Goodings, Marguerite Van Die, and Don Matheson.

I wish also to thank Douglas John Hall, who has been a

trustworthy guide in so much of my learning. It was through his interest in the subject of stewardship that I was initially introduced to this field of church work and research.

Most recently I have reason to acknowledge the support of the members of the congregation of Centenary-Queen Square United Church in Saint John, New Brunswick. They have been patient with my absences when I have travelled to present seminars and to lead worship in stewardship events. Their keen questions in our Bible study groups are never far from my mind as I try to respond to the challenges of their lives through the pages of this book.

The editors and promoters of The United Church Publishing House have been both kind and inspired in their direction.

Finally I want to thank my partner and companion, Kelly Higgins. Her sensitive soul and sharp intuition have inspired and clarified many of the ideas that eventually found their way into this book.

Foreword

Chris Levan has been deeply immersed in theological and practical concerns related to Christian stewardship for a number of years. He served as a major presenter at the 1992 Colloquy for Theological Educators, held at St. Paul's United College in Waterloo, Ontario, and sponsored by the Ecumenical Center for Stewardship Studies (ECSS). He also served as worship leader at one of the 1992 Conferences on Stewardship in the Small Membership Congregation, also sponsored by ECSS.

In *The Dancing Steward*, both theological and practical dimensions of Christian stewardship are reflected. Levan combines biblical stories and images that illumine our understanding of Christian stewardship with powerful and illustrative stories from his own experience. He notes the dissonance between gospel and reality that too frequently occurs and observes that even when our bellies are filled to overflowing, we can be empty in our souls. Levan has provided a guide to those who seek to bring harmony to this dissonance.

Using the ethic of relinquishment, understood both as spiritual journey and creative challenge, Chris frames his work in three workshops. The first workshop establishes a biblical base for the ethic of relinquishment. The rich ruler of the synoptic Gospels is presented as a paradigm of stewardship trends within the late twentieth century. Attention is also given to the difficulty of relinquishing when we are part of a consumer society. The dilemma of "letting go" is real.

In the second workshop, Levan maintains that conversion of the spirit takes place through solidarity with the marginalized. The well-known parable of the division of the sheep and goats (Matt. 25) is used to apply theories of liberation theology to the question of Christian stewardship within a North American context. The third workshop explores the human need for hope and notes that relinquishment should be done with purpose and hope.

Levan views relinquishment as a natural pre-condition of Christian discipleship; indeed, even the essence of faith. It is not merely a faddish spiritual technique that will quickly fade away. In stating this, however, Levan is careful to point out that the ethic of relinquishment has its dangers and cautions. Important conditions and caveats are noted.

Levan also deals with the question of how you give it all away. In his answer, he deals with both the practical and spiritual dimensions. The gospel message, he states, is unequivocal: Christian discipleship begins with a genuine relinquishment.

Let it be noted that guilt is not the motivating force for genuine relinquishment. Relinquishment, in and of itself, is not redemptive. Rather, a "second conversion," a spiritual, emotional, and intellectual turning about is experienced—a confrontation with a God who loves and a decision to live differently. It is a liberation from the reigning, grasping predisposition of our acquisitive world. Relinquishment is linked with solidarity; letting go to stand with the marginalized. Above all, states Levan, relinquishment is impossible without the action of God.

Finally, Levan describes relinquishment, solidarity, and expectancy as intertwined in an exhilarating dance. The dance of stewardship is circular. When we come back to where we started, we find there is more to learn. The vision is breathtaking. The title "The Dancing Steward" is indeed appropriate.

This book contains two plays that I have had the privilege of seeing performed. Their effect on the audience was stunning. They are powerful. I would recommend their use with groups in the church.

The Dancing Steward will become an important landmark in the history of Christian stewardship in North America. Our thanks go to Chris Levan.

Ronald E. Vallet
Executive Director
Ecumenical Center for Stewardship Studies

Introduction

Prosperity and Poverty: The Dilemma of the Affluent

What is the most shocking realization of all, however, is that absolute poverty and its deprivations are entirely unnecessary. Food supply in the world exceeds population.... There is sufficient technology to supply clean water systems and sanitation systems for the present world population. Yet 800 million persons continue to live in conditions that none of us would ever willingly choose.

— Elizabeth Morgan et al. 1989, 42-43

It's Christmas Eve in Deerfield Beach, Florida. Hot? I should say so! Much too hot for a child of the north. How can I touch the mystery of "God with us" when there's no snow, no sleigh bells jingling, no chestnuts roasting on an open fire? Lemonade by the pool and waving palm trees simply don't do it! They can't reproduce that rich soil in which the dream of Christmas grows.

I ask myself: Where is the crisp sparkle of expectation, the twinkling snap of anticipation? Where is the centuries-old light of candles shining from the frosted edges of my mind, a light that lifts back the veil of time to reveal timeless secrets? I feel nothing here. Nothing!

This must be a new production of the theatre of the absurd; an incongruous mixture of hopes and dreams. My Christmas yearn-

1

ings are to Florida what whipping cream is to a hot dog—embarrassingly and disappointingly out of place. Picture it: I am relaxing in an outdoor pool the temperature of warm soup, looking across trimmed lawns, watching people turn on festive lights that will never be reflected by snow. I feel alien, out of place, a stranger in a foreign land. My discomfort increases when we go for Christmas dinner.

One hundred people, including our table of four, are crammed into the tiny lobby of the Waterfall Inn. Of course, everyone has a reservation for five o'clock. We're here to enjoy the blessing of what is close to being a sacramental meal in this culture, the one where families let go of sadness and rejoice in common good fortune. "God bless us, every one," as Tiny Tim says.

No one is being seated, so we all mill about, talking and complaining at the same time. The commotion is indescribable. Red-faced men, bolstered by martinis, mutter oaths, and stylish women fume under their pampered facades. Children run among our legs as if they are squirrels and we are trees. What a great game ... for squirrels. Crusty old elms and heavy oaks creak and moan at the bother of it all, while little creatures scramble under limb and past trunk. Cane-toting elders pace uncomfortably about the edges of our discontent—the children's make-believe forest—looking for seats that do not exist.

Above the ever-increasing noise of the crowd, the brash voice of the *maitre d'* calls out seating arrangements with the indifference of an overworked taxi driver: "Jones for three"; "Smith for five"; "Levan for four." That's us. Finally!

The mayhem in the lobby disperses the last traces of Christmas spirit lingering in my heart. As I sit down to eat, I surrender to the absurdity of it all. It's simpler and less painful that way. With no expectations, there's no grief. Here we are celebrating "Peace on earth and good will to all people," while we rubberneck around to see who is eating what. And all the while we're complaining about the service and badgering the exhausted waitresses for more turkey.

I listen to the murmurs of indulgence and cynicism as we

gossip about the other noisy patrons and look down on their foolish antics. The dissonance between gospel and reality could not be more jarring. I am both fascinated and depressed.

In the midst of our luxuriant, ludicrous feasting stands a mechanical Santa Claus. Throughout the entire evening, with feet astride the modulated, artificial waterfall from which the restaurant takes its name, he bows and extends his hands, bestowing a blessing on our celebration. I sit facing this mechanical marvel, and as I watch, I notice how my interpretation of his gestures changes with my mood.

While we sip cocktails, Santa is jovial, the classic Kris Kringle, shouting out in a rich, plum-pudding tone: "Ho! Ho! Ho!" He's as merry as any self-respecting Santa Claus should be.

When the soup and entrée are served, his voice becomes less resonant, less mirthful. Now it's a touch strident, and I imagine him speaking, not from among the sweet-smelling plastic flowers, but rather from among the beaten, sweating, starving people of this world, begging for food: "Oh, please! Oh, please! Oh, please!"

The mashed potatoes weigh heavily in my stomach. The luscious spoonfuls of stuffing stick in my throat, mocking my Yuletide gestures of charity. Here Santa pleads for food for the hungry, and I continue to gorge, incapable of stopping the flow of food to my mouth, unable to imagine what else I might do.

Dessert arrives. I hear another voice coming from our never-ceasing, ever-bowing host. He's angry. With hands reaching out, dipping low, he sneers: "Oh, bug off! Oh, bug off! Oh, bug off!" The red-suited mannequin rains down judgement upon us and our feast. Could this be the prophet Amos, disguised as jolly old Saint Nick? I hear the ancient words: "Thus says the Lord. I hate, I despise your feast days. I take no delight in your solemn assemblies" (Amos 5:21, paraphrase).

We pay and leave, our bellies filled to overflowing with turkey and pie. But we are empty in our souls. Walking from the restaurant, I'm confused. I feel guilty and very disturbed. It is not the shallowness of our merriment that troubles me, even though my festive expectations have not been met. Rather, it is the inevitable drift of Santa's message that has rattled my sense of tranquillity and balance. It unnerves me—the movement from banal acquiescence to stubborn resistance, from slavish servitude to outright rebellion. Is this the end of it all? Will an obese world never learn of its oppressive consumption? And if we eventually discover our greed, will it be too late? Will our current indifference fire the flames of revolt until nothing will quench their fury?

Looking at our world, I wonder if we, the affluent people, are not trapped by our own riches and are unable to respond to the cries of the marginalized because we just cannot imagine ourselves in that world. Is the only solution a violent confrontation between the rich and poor of this planet, between the overfed patrons and the overworked servants? During the festive season, when charity flows more freely, I ask how the "haves" could give to the "have nots," so that true peace and good will can come down to earth.

These are the questions provoked by that silent Kris Kringle. Indeed, I suggest that they are the primary questions facing the powerful and wealthy peoples of this day. Now that the more precarious obstacles to an East-West dialogue have been removed, the dangers inherent in the gulf that separates North and South are more apparent. How can the affluent share their wealth?

While reading the following chapters, I ask you to remember the questions raised by the Floridian Santa Claus, because they are the stimulus to rethinking the meaning of Christian stewardship lifestyles for people of the First World. They express the urgency of our situation. We are rich, healthy, and well fed, while most people of the world are poor, sick, and starving. UNICEF statistics indicate that in the time it has taken you to read these few pages (How long has it been? Five minutes?), 135 children have died for lack of the earth's most abundant resource: clean water.

In that well-appointed restaurant, and many times since, I have asked: "Am I the keeper of my brother and sister? What does their great need mean to me?"

I have written this book out of a deep and growing sense of urgency. This is not a theoretical treatise on the hypothetical dilemmas of Christian stewardship; one you can pick up at your leisure. It is a plea for understanding and action. At every corner we face the marginalized. They crowd our city sidewalks and haunt our soup kitchens. Their plight fills the nightly news as they walk the thin line between survival and destitution, while our social "safety nets" shrink. A day hardly passes without the crying desperation of the poor in Africa or Asia or Latin America being brought right into our living rooms. "What therefore must I do?" That is my cry.

Is this cry yours? Are you searching for an answer to the predicament of your affluence? After you've been approached by the third homeless person in as many blocks, do you ask "What must I do?" It is in answer to that question that I have written this book.

I begin my exploration of these questions with the assumption that the lot of the destitute will not improve unless the economic ordering of the planet shifts in their favour. At some point, if we are to avoid civil strife, the affluent must give up or relinquish some of their grasp upon power and privilege, so that those marginal to the sources of economic power can gain some semblance of self-sufficiency.

Not being an economist, I recognize that I am prone to an over-simplification of a complicated financial equation. However, the general movement towards an equitable economic order has been obvious for several decades. The North will have to allow the South to dictate higher prices for its natural resources. No matter how we slice it, the North will have to share its power. The rich must learn to "let go" if the poor are to receive.

Power is rarely transferred easily. This is as clear in a microcosm as it is in a macrocosm. Think of a parent-child relationship. How does the mother give control to the daughter who wishes to stay out at a dance? There is the obvious temptation of paternalism, in which we smother our offspring in "good" advice and "helpful" gestures, covertly designed to keep us in the driver's seat. There is the opposite temptation of abdication, in which we leave our children to their own devices: "Go ahead, make a mess of your life. See if I care."

Similar dynamics are evident in the dilemma of the affluent who wish to share their power in an equitable fashion with the marginalized. We fall prey to the political form of paternalism—colonialism or neo-colonialism—and we are sorely tempted to abdicate our role in world development, blaming the victims for their own lack of short-term success.

As well as questions of a political and economic nature, the sharing of wealth raises conundrums of another order, deeper and more philosophical. Will the powerful willingly let go of their power? Marxist analysis argues that the allure of wealth and private property are too enticing. Human beings will not willingly relinquish power. If that is true, then this entire exercise is futile. It would be better to set this book aside and read a manual on social revolt.

A capitalist would maintain that any relinquishing of power is unnecessary, since the laws of economics will eventually redress any grave imbalance between rich and poor. Better to look over *The Financial Post*.

A Christian might well suggest that there are two dimensions to the question of sharing power and resources; that is, to the question of stewardship. On the one hand, there is the issue of human free will. Perhaps human beings simply don't have the heart for relinquishment. On our own, we can't will ourselves to be less powerful than we are. If this is the case, stewardship becomes a matter of the spirit—it calls for conversion. On the other hand, our "tight" stewardship may indicate a lack of imagination. We cannot picture what such a divested lifestyle would look like, so we fear it and ignore the call to a new way of being a disciple.

On a personal level (at some point all demands of stewardship become subjective), I often ask myself if I can or even should give it all away and become as the poor. In my more radical moments, this path is appealing: "Fight the good fight"; stand at the cross of Jesus! However, this path has its own complications. If I decide to relinquish all, am I allowed to decide that for my children and my partner as well?

Moreover, relinquishment is not so simple, since I "have" more than money and financial assets. If I am to give for the sake of an equitable distribution of the earth's resources, what do I do with those things that I cannot give away but that also contribute to my wealth and status, i.e., my university degrees, business contacts, social standing accrued through family name or prior accomplishments? How do I share all those things?

Then, in my more cynical moments, when the shine has worn off the gospel's call, I wonder if divestment of any kind is really effective. Will the poor really benefit if I give away all that I have? Besides, do I really need to take all these stewardship imperatives with such seriousness? Will my world fall apart if I do nothing at all? Are these your questions too? I hope so since they are the primary focus of what follows.

Initially I thought it was wildly ironic and even misguided to write on the topic of Christian stewardship for a people (I include myself as a charter member of this group) who are so burdened by possessions that they must build bigger and bigger two-car garages in which to store it all. What can we possibly want to hear about stewardship and the giving away of God's gifts? After all, we're so busy collecting "stuff" that we don't have time to reflect on any other course of action.

Upon reflection, I decided that appropriating a healthy and imaginative attitude towards Christian stewardship is, in fact, the primary issue facing affluent North American Christians. It is the very essence of our faith journey. I consider it the start of our theology of liberation.

If there is a fundamental motivating thesis for this book it is that Christian stewardship in the context of a male-dominated, affluent society requires a judicious appropriation of the ethic of relinquishment, relinquishment understood as both spiritual journey and creative challenge. Letting go may not be the first or final step, but it is a fundamental one for the well endowed.

7

In order to explore this thesis, I have laid out three workshops on stewardship lifestyles. Each reflects a gospel story. I use the term "workshop" advisedly. In the time of Jesus, there were no such events, but his telling of parables and his discussions with others served the same function. Each workshop in the following pages begins with a specific parable or story on a distinct theme of stewardship lifestyles.

In the first workshop, I begin by establishing a biblical base for the ethic of relinquishment. In chapter 1, I unravel the parable of the rich ruler of the synoptic Gospels—one who would possess eternal life. He is the paradigm of current stewardship trends within our late twentieth-century context. Chapter 2 is playful. In fact, it is a modern adaptation of the rich young ruler's dilemma of letting go.

I then initiate the debate on relinquishment by pointing out that self-identity and the spirit of possession are closely linked within the consumer society and explaining why relinquishment is difficult. The debate on the difficulty of relinquishment continues with an examination of the religious motivation to possess and how God is used to legitimate our possessiveness. The inadequacies of some traditional theological positions concerning possessions lead quite naturally to questions of conversion. How can the possessing spirit find fulfilment and freedom? How is repentance or a radical turnaround possible?

In a second "workshop," I argue that this conversion takes place through solidarity with the marginalized. Using the well-known judgement parable of the division of sheep and goats found in Matthew 25:31-44, I apply some theories of liberation theology to the question of North American stewardship. Appropriate relinquishment in our context is preceded by an act of commitment to and for the crucified ones of this planet. "Letting go" is made possible because of God's gracious and beckoning presence among the dispossessed. Again, I have included a play to illustrate this fact.

The third workshop explores the human need for expectancy. "Letting go" is a lonely affair. How can we do it with purpose and hope? Some concrete examples of how this relinquishment might take place both in our individual lives and in the life of the community of faith are given, along with an examination of the challenges and the dangers of an ethic of relinquishment as it might be employed in the North American church. All too often the exaltation of "letting go" has been used to perpetuate bondage and abuse. Given the dangers of distorting an ethic of relinquishment, it must be proposed and undertaken with great care.

I have chosen this particular order of themes because it is a pattern suggested by the natural flow of conversion. Conversion begins with a confrontation that jars our preconceived positions, beliefs, and thoughts. This encounter leads naturally to a period of "letting go" of false ideas and dreams and a strong passion to live according to our new insights. This passion brings us into contact with others who share our fervour. Together we outline our dreams and live our hopes.

Most believers move from charity to justice in the manner I have outlined. Moreover, this thematic pattern captures the rhythm of Christian theology—the road from the cross to the empty tomb, from Good Friday to Easter morning. If you look at Matthew 16:24-25, you will see the same pattern: "If any would come after me, let that one deny self, take up his or her cross and follow me."

While the following chapters are of considerable theoretical content, the directed personal reflection, the study questions, and the practical exercises at the end of each chapter will guide the reader to some concrete applications of these theories, both for the individual and for local church bodies.

An introduction should introduce, so before ending this one, there are some autobiographical comments to be made. I have fashioned them somewhat as a confession and somewhat as an autobiographical footnote.

Even though I write about need, destitution, poverty, and oppression, I want to make clear that I have not suffered these things. I will not pretend that I am one of the dispossessed. On the contrary, being educated past high school and endowed with the privileges and confidence of a middle-class heritage, being straight, well employed, white, and male, there is no question that I am one with the powerful of this world. These sociological factors mean that no matter what I do with my life, I will always have a place among the influential, even when they don't want me.

While I'm not proud of my station, neither can I deny it. Power, even when unsolicited, imposes a certain responsibility on those who hold it. Recognizing and "letting go" of the inappropriate monopoly of power is in fact the proper business of the affluent, one that requires as much courage as a liberation struggle to achieve power.

In this regard, it is especially to the well-endowed and influential people like myself that Jesus speaks, when he says, "When a man or woman has a great deal given to him or her, a great deal will be demanded of that one" (Luke 12:48, paraphrase). This book is a contribution to the debate over an appropriate theology for the non-poor. The poverty-stricken peoples of Latin America have developed a theology of liberation. I am proposing a theology of relinquishment as the indigenous theology for the white, affluent, male-dominated North American society.

Following directly from this first confession is a second one. I am caught. Even while I resist the consumptive acquisitiveness of this culture, I am captive to it. In the context of my Floridian experience I can only paraphrase what Isaiah said so clearly: "I am a man of bloated belly and I dwell in the midst of a people with bloated bellies" (Isa. 6:5).

While none of us is personally responsible for the horrendous inequality between possessors and the dispossessed, we cannot help but feel caught in a darkening spiral of consumption that is eating away at the healthy fibres of human existence on this planet. The holes in the ozone layer, the polluted rivers, the greenhouse effect, all eventually come back to our lifestyle, our ever-expanding appetite for what the earth provides in limited quantities. We are the world's problem.

Most of us will admit that it is not easy being the problem.

We'd much rather be the solution, the saviour, the rescuer, the competent professional, the conflict manager. Very rarely do we recognize ourselves as the abuser, the miser, the one who needs saving, the overfed.

A colleague once posted a sign outside his door that said: "The world can no longer afford the rich." That is the humbling reality with which the affluent North American must live. We are the leeches on the body of the earth. Our extravagance and opulence have cost creation much. Isn't it true that the "developed" world has treated the earth like its own private party room, living as if the festivities would go on forever? In these last years of the twentieth century, we have discovered much to our surprise and consternation that the party is over and that it's time to pay the bill. Who's going to pick up the tab? The problem with settling the account is that the possessors have lived so long on material and spiritual loans that we have nothing with which to settle our debts.

There is another way in which we are caught. In many ways, all North Americans live in Florida. It's that Disneyland life sold in shopping malls across the continent. We all breath it in, we all buy it. Let's not fool ourselves; the Floridian life is found even at the local store down the street. We are captivated by it—the good life on display, infinitely new, always improving, and incredibly empty. It's an addiction. We can't stop ourselves, we eat it up as if it were mid-afternoon soap operas. It's a fascinating, trivialized life, lived at a desperate pitch, without purpose, an existence covered with glitz and suntan oil. How can we escape it?

Is there any way to get free? Should we give up in despair? I think not. While we are capable of great ecological destruction and racial oppression and have a seemingly endless appetite for possessing, nevertheless we know ourselves to be a forgiven people who live by grace. Kept from false pride and false despair by this gift of grace, we can move beyond confession to action. This may sound trite when written so boldly, but I trust this entire text will flesh out the affirmation of grace.

As a consequence of grace, believers sense that they are forgiven, set free from the weight of guilt for a purpose. There is a "for" added to the Christian understanding of freedom. We are set free for something, for some purpose, for someone. The theme behind the parable of the talents found in Matthew 25:14ff is instructive at this point. While some Christians have construed the message of the story of the three servants and their varying trust funds to be a thinly veiled justification for usury and market capitalism, I would argue that its central message is about risk. God's stewards are not meant to hoard the master's gifts, to keep them sheltered and protected, but to risk them. Blessed is the one who risks what the Creator has bestowed—who being set free, risks all to liberate others.

The non-poor, the powerful, are called upon to know their power, to be humble before their culpability, but finally to be prepared to risk their gifts and their lives. Without such a purpose, our lives as Christians would be meaningless.

Experiential Learning

1. The next time you go to a restaurant, ask the waitress what it's like to serve people food. Do servers get a chance to eat? Do they have to pay for it themselves? How are they treated by customers? How is serving food in a restaurant different from serving food at home?

2. Watch the movie *Gandhi*. Is relinquishment a dream reserved for saints? Can ordinary people do it?

Questions for Discussion

1. Do you know someone who is poor? Did or do you live through it yourself? Why are there hungry and homeless people? Who or what is to blame?

2. What do you think when you go to the shopping mall? Is it the modern equivalent of the town square? Is shopping there

different than it used to be? What are the primary messages you read and hear in your experience of the shopping centre?

3. Does the Bible tell us anything about shopping and buying? Are there any guidelines? Look at Amos 7:1-8. What does the prophet imply about economic practices? Read Deuteronomy 15:1-10 and ask what sort of vision this passage holds for the consumer society.

Chapter One

The Primary Stewardship Question for the Affluent and Powerful

Did you not come naked from the womb? Will you not return naked into the earth? Where then did you have all your present possessions?

—Basil the Great (Avila 1983, 49)

Introduction

Most Christians associate the word "stewardship" with church fund-raising; a fancy word used to sanctify the rather mundane task of securing enough dollars to finance church activities. Large churches may have "stewardship" committees and campaigns for the funding of their many programmes. However, in the small membership church, stewardship is even further reduced to describe the constant grind of raising the minister's salary.

On the other end of the scale from this narrow vision of stewardship, some theologians and church leaders have interpreted it to be an attitude or perspective through which to view the whole religious exercise. To be Christian is to be a steward and to be a steward is to be involved in the mission of God in this world.

Which definition is correct? Is stewardship only the collection of money or is it the Christian disciple's attitude towards the whole of creation? While each of these notions has merit and biblical foundations, and while they ought to be held in a creative tension—the broad vision informing the daily management of God's gifts and and the raising of money—it has been my experience that they are usually kept separate in the day to day reality of church life.

In theory, we accent both (stewardship as the nurturing of faithful giving and stewardship as discipleship), but in practice, Christian communities have built very few bridges between the task of ecclesiastical fund raising and the striving to live "stewardly" lives. We can talk the talk, but how do we walk the walk? How do we get from money to lifestyle in a truly meaningful way?

Is it possible to visualize how we can move from fund raising to living a new life as a community of disciples? Where is the bridge? I propose to explore one bridge between these two poles of Christian stewardship by speaking about stewardship "lifestyles" and, more specifically, by examining the notion of possession.

Since our North American world seems almost fixated on "having" and "holding," it makes sense that any discussion of possessions should begin with an examination of the consuming spirit, the passion to own, our soul-felt urge to "have." Isn't this the middle point between money and lifestyle, the place where "the rubber hits the road"? Perhaps if we unravel our need to possess we can understand the radical claims of stewardship within the life of Christian discipleship.

Workshop One: Learning to Let Go

While some may dispute it, I suggest that the first workshop on Christian stewardship lifestyles was held on the dusty road between the scattered villages of Samaria and the ancient city of Jerusalem. Granted, in those days workshops were lean affairs. There wasn't much advance publicity. Travel vouchers, styrofoam cups, flip charts and conference centres were non-existent. People just waited for a wise leader to pass by and then followed him or her for a time—weeks, months, even years—trying to glean a portion of wisdom. Unlike our modern world, the ancients understood that wisdom was available only to those who took time to journey into the unknown. It could not be purchased in two-day seminar chunks.

On this occasion, the workshop leader was a Nazarene peasant called Jesus. Well known for his special effects and rather outlandish and subversive ideas, he promised to be the "learning event" of the season. Looking at the great rabbi with post-resurrection eyes, we take his popularity for granted. We never ask ourselves why this particular messiah figure gained so much favour with the people. Let's explore that question now.

Why was the son of a Galilean woodworker so unique as a teacher? Perhaps it was Christ's compassion for the crowd, for the people who lived on the fringes of society, the rejected and shunned. Coming from a marginal town himself, Jesus may have had that special "common touch" born of personal experience.

Perhaps the master's disarming humility or his healing power drew the ever-increasing audiences. Everyone loves a good doctor. Why wouldn't crowds flock to the new healer in town? There was certainly a crying need.

No doubt Jesus' sharp but never bitter wit was attractive. Who could miss his sharp-edged and delightful sense of the sacrilegious, jabs at the establishment that brought even the religious elite to a new awareness of their destructive self-righteousness?

Did the carpenter's popularity rest with his intellect, with a depth of wisdom that uncovered deep and forgotten secrets of human existence? What about his piety? Surely his oneness with the Creator was an impressive gift.

Certainly the master's miracles had popular appeal. No one else could make five loaves and two fishes go so far. No wonder the hungry masses gathered around him. But whatever the great teacher's touch, the Christian scriptures are primarily a response to the uniqueness that was and is Jesus of Nazareth.

In this book, I want to focus on the eloquence of Jesus, on his vocation as a story-teller. His genius in this regard is perhaps without equal in the history of human civilization. Simple tales of common experience burst into flame through his gift of parable. Planted seeds, helpful shepherds, lost coins, fishing nets; these are simple, almost banal, objects. Yet, we now recognize them as the bearers of the most profound truths, not only about Christian faith, but about human existence in general.

Crowds flocked to hear Jesus weave his tales and many were converted to a new way of living because of his parables. They forsook their pasts and their possessions in order to be his disciples. Mary's son accomplished all of this without the conveniences of modern audio-visual equipment.

While the simplicity of his stories is remarkable, I believe his true genius is evident in what modern pedagogues might call the real-life role plays that he summoned forth from the people. Jesus often developed his story, the truth of a parable, out of the very people he faced. The local townsfolk began to tell the master's story, modelling the truth of his sayings by their very actions and deeds.

Children pushed forward in their innocence and enthusiasm, seeking only a blessing. In so doing, they embodied the message of the reign of God: that only those who are unpretentious, who seek only to receive a word of grace, who unconsciously love life, can be found by God. Money-changers repented and gave back the money they extorted, incarnating a prophetic parable concerning the abuse of privilege and the power of disarming forgiveness. Living out the story, fishers left their nets and women gave of their household budgets to promote the ministry of Jesus, all giving ample testimony to the cost of discipleship.

Surely these living lessons were impressive. They spoke eloquently of the influence and truth that was the rabbi of Galilee. They formed a body of workshops through which people learned and grew. They can still teach us today.

The first stewardship workshop had such an embodiment of the central message as its theme presentation. The story is found in all the synoptic Gospels, but I will concentrate on Luke's version (Luke 18). You could perhaps read it now to refresh your memory.

It begins in an unassuming manner. The crowd is gathered around Jesus. Children are bouncing on the master's knee. You can hear the general commotion, approving grunts and whispered awe. Jesus begins to talk and a hush descends. The town square listens. The rabbi relates a tale about a wicked judge and a pestering widow that brims over with wit and wisdom. He tells how the powerless outcast outsmarts the powerful judge of righteousness.

Then Jesus directs a few discomforting words to the local religious ones, the ones who do not think they need to repent. Can you hear him? "Do you think that you righteous people will find salvation? Does the keeping of a few laws ensure right relationships? Does it ensure the establishment of God's shalom?"

Perhaps it was this last point, perhaps it was entirely unrelated to the previous stories, but out of the crowd steps the stewardship parable *par excellence*. Now we get to the theme address of that first stewardship workshop.

A wealthy man comes forward to speak. Recognizing his position, the disciples make way and he confronts Jesus face to face. There is no evidence in Luke that the man is "young." This is Matthew's suggestion (Matt. 19:20). The reader is not told of the man's lineage or specific occupation. Luke points out only that he is a member of one of the leading aristocratic families of the region. Here is the Palestinian equivalent of a town judge, university professor, bank manager, and prize fighter all rolled up into one person.

It would be wise for us, the privileged ones of North America, to examine this man carefully, for we are to our society what he was to his. He had status. He was a "good" person, the one everyone wanted on their board of directors. He would be called on to sit at the table of honour for sports banquets and to give the dedication address for the new senior's complex. This ruler had it all—almost. He didn't have the assurance of eternity.

I wonder about his motives. Why does this man want to speak to Jesus? Is he frightened or proud? Is he truly searching or only amusing himself? Is he playing with a powerless intruder like a cat plays with a mouse, just waiting for the right moment to pounce? Was he speaking for himself out of his own personal sense of urgency or was he primed by the town leaders who sought to buttress their religious authority against the intrusion of this itinerant preacher? Did the local bourgeoisie pool their ideas, make a motion, and send forth their champion to do battle with the upstart evangelist who was upsetting the trusted religious order and meddling in the time-honoured economic structures of village life?

While there is no historical evidence with which to respond to these questions, I do believe that the man confronting Jesus speaks for others as well as for himself. His real quest goes far beyond the particulars of a single question. His is the voice of privilege and power. His is a voice that expects to be heard, a voice that desires much.

How does this town ruler begin? He addresses Jesus as "Good master." Isn't that typical! Power is always so polite—at first. It can afford to be, since it's in control. After money, we possessors believe most in propriety, in the general acknowledgement that things are the way they should be. To disrupt the status quo, even if it is merely through abrupt or pointed language, is treasonous, and we resent it. So the ruler begins his question with a polite nod, which reinforces his position.

"Good master, what must I do to inherit eternal life?"

Without a doubt, that is the most profound and the most misleading of all human questions; profound, because it describes the depth of human yearning for that which defies and overcomes the ambiguity and finiteness of existence, misleading because it assumes that such a precious commodity as eternal life can be held or possessed in some way. Many conflicts and wars have resulted from both the depth and danger of that question.

The response of Jesus to the aristocrat's quest for the eternal is well known. Jesus asks the ruler about his religious observance, and upon discovering that the man believes that he has kept all the commandments, Jesus tells him that he lacks ones thing: "Go sell all you have and give to the poor and then come and be my disciple." And then...

There must have been a pregnant pause right at this point. Can you feel the tension, the tingling drama of this moment? Jesus is meeting this man head on and saying, essentially, "There's the challenge. You want eternal life. Right, then, here it is, but first get rid of everything you own."

So we are all hushed. What will he do? Is the goal worth it? All the eyes of the townsfolk are on the town aristocrat. Now is the time for truth! How will he choose? Alas, the spirit withers and the hope fades. The *kairos* moment passes and the man turns away sorrowful for, according to Luke, "he had many possessions."

From our perspective as post-resurrection Christians, we might ask, "Why did he not give it all away?" It was such a small request when viewed in the context of all the events that have happened since. What significance is the small fortune of one man in a marginal town in a marginal country in the first-century Roman empire, which itself became but a footnote in the span of human history? What is that paltry sum of money when compared with the prize of eternal life? The opportunity to be a disciple of Jesus, to actually walk in his footsteps—how many modern Christians would give everything they have and hold to receive that gift? How can it compare to earthly chattel?

Nevertheless, we should not be too hard on Luke's town ruler. We have the same opportunity presented to us each day when we meet the panhandler or homeless stranger. Most Christians agree with the town aristocrat—the price is too high—and we walk away.

Gazing at the slightly stooped shoulders of that sad man as he walked back toward his treasure, back into his well-oiled existence, we might ask again about his motives. Was he genuine, but hopelessly naive in his quest for the eternal? Was he essentially an innocent who asked for what cannot be given? Or was he, in fact, insecure, dishonest, and acquisitive, basically a greedy man? While he was obviously tinged with a bit of all these characteristics (as are we who search for the same thing), the author of Luke appears to direct his readers towards the latter possibilities. Here is a man of wealth trying to add one last possession, the ultimate "bobble" to his eathly substance. Imagine: to grasp the gift of eternal life, to possess the infinite!

The words of Jesus echo in his thoughts as he moves back from the crowd. "You must give away everything you possess." Regrettably, the rich man couldn't do it.

Listening to that stark command through the acquisitive sensitivities of the North American culture and a long tradition of spiritualizing biblical theology, Christians make excuses for the rich ruler: Jesus didn't really intend that his words be taken literally; he was simply putting the man's discipleship to the test, a first-century version of career assessment planning. Believers of this persuasion argue that Jesus did not expect his instructions to the rich ruler to be legalistically or universally interpreted. For this particular individual, riches were a stumbling block, but many rich people have been and are faithful followers of the teacher from Nazareth. The real barrier, therefore, is spiritual, not material, i.e., the ruler's faithfulness and lack of trust. If only he had more of each, the whole question of material goods would never have arisen.

There is a good deal of truth in this rationalization, which I hope to illustrate in subsequent chapters of this book. Physical objects in and of themselves are not the chief stumbling block of discipleship. Rather the problem is the peculiar possessing spirit that seeks to cling to the material, imputing to it an eternal significance which derails our noblest intentions. We cannot separate holding from having, control from ownership. This disrupts the quest for the eternal in our midst.

While I want to explore the emotional and spiritual dimensions of the ethic of possessing, I first want to state, in as unrelenting a manner as possible, that Jesus meant exactly what he said! It would be terribly unjust both to the text and to the testimony of the early church if this point were not absolutely clear. Despite other allusions he might have wanted to make, Jesus was definitely claiming that material possessions are a dead end on the road to the realm of God. Read my lips: "You must give away everything you possess."

21

Apart from its continuity with other sayings of Jesus (in Matthew 5, 6, 7, for example), evidence for this literal interpretation is offered in Mark's version of the story. After the ruler asks his questions, Mark adds this footnote: "Jesus looked steadily at him and loved him" (Mark 10:21). This commentary on Jesus' motives indicates that his command to "sell everything" was not a clever trick or test. Here is a genuine word, spoken in love. Jesus was not playing a mind game. He told the wealthy man exactly what was required. Riches, actual cash in the bank, assets, houses, cars, chariots, all you possess will hold you back from entering the realm of God.

Thus, there was never a more puzzled band of workshop participants than those first few disciples who listened as Jesus went on to explain the impossible possibility of his demands: "It is easier for a camel to go through the eye of a needle than for a rich man to enter the realm of God" (Mark 10:25).

"It can't be done!" they cried. They were right! You can't get a camel through the eye of a needle. You can't get a rich person into God's reign. No matter how ingenious you are, no matter how fast you drive it, you can't get a Cadillac through a revolving door, at least not without leaving most of the Cadillac outside.

Possessions keep the disciple from entering the pathway to eternal life—the depth of transcendence waiting behind daily living and beyond death. The prophetic imaginings of the Bible and the writings of early church leaders reiterate the message of this living parable. Objects, if they become possessions or idols, are not to be trusted. Private ownership is particularly suspect and to be discouraged as illusory and potentially idolatrous. Even though physical items on their own are not the chief problem, nevertheless the insecure heart sees an opportunity for protective wholeness in the possession of material goods. Jesus and the prophets understood that the acquisition of great riches is the result of a dream that stretches well beyond the mere objects of ownership. The possession of objects is simply the means of attaining an absolute state of wholeness and freedom from imperfection, pain, and discomfort.

The story of the town aristocrat is the first and foundational stewardship workshop for the North American context because it captures our predicament so well. Like many, I long for completion and a sense of security. The more I strive to arrive at a state of wholeness through the acquisition of things, the more I realize that it's not for sale. It can't be bought or held. In my more sane, though often fleeting, moments, I glimpse the exact opposite: that wholeness is a state of being that comes only when we let go. But I can't let go! Unfortunately, I have been taught to hang on. Letting go equals giving in—surrendering—being a coward, a soft touch.

Hence, the possession of material objects figures in the ironic paradox of our North American life: the desperate passion to have and to hold and the well-known shallowness of this dream. This is the paradox of our patriarchal culture. From my birth onward, I have been taught that possessions and possessing are vital to my existence. I've also learned that nothing is readily "mine." Possession is a hollow myth.

Nevertheless, once the primacy of possessing and owning is accepted, it is quite difficult to let go. In the following chapter, we will playfully explore this predicament.

Experiential Learning

1. Watch one hour of prime-time television programming on any major   network and record what images, values, and ideas are associated with possessions. Make a list and compare them to the Christian mission found in Luke 4:18.

2. Read newspaper advertisements for automobiles and beer. What are they really selling? Why would we want to buy these things?

3. Stand at the intersection of two busy streets in a major urban centre at noon hour and do a survey. Ask only one question:

What do you want most in life? If you do this as a group you may get some very revealing results.

Questions for Discussion

1. What do we want most in life?

2. What does it mean to possess something?

3. What does the Bible say about ownership?

4. Is the young ruler of Luke's gospel similar to us in any way?

5. What keeps you from being a disciple of Jesus, from selling all you have to follow Christ?

6. If your house were burning and you could save only one thing, what would it be? Why is this one thing important? Could you give it away for the sake of Christ's mission in the world?

Chapter Two

Holding On to Letting Go

*In untroubled times only extraordinary men and women
radically question the consensus reality. However in troubled
times the number of people thrown into psychological turmoil
and radical questioning increases. And that of course, is our
present condition.*

—Sam Keen 1991, 126

Introduction

Some men are very "tight." Some would say we are uptight or
tight fisted, but I refer the simpler version. We are tight. We grow
up learning to hold on, to possess, to grasp, and achieve. We
incarnate the North American context, which also defines itself
according to its "tightness"—its ability to have and hold whatever it prizes.

The following play begins to explore the paradox of how
much we want to hang on and how much we need to let go. Read
it out loud or act it out with others or try a group reading in
which everyone takes a part. It's marvellous how drama comes
alive when we hear it and give life to its characters. Above all,
play with it and enjoy it. Let loose! For me, play is the one place
where I can relax my possessive spirit enough to see the possibilities inherent in letting go.

There are two people hanging on to a rope, branch or board, symbolizing leaves hanging on a tree. It is spring.

JOHN: Burrrhhh. That was a cold one.

JEFF: *(yawning)* What?

JOHN: I said that was a cold one.

JEFF: A cold what?

JOHN: A cold ... a cold ... I don't know. Just a cold "one." You know ... what we just went through.

JEFF: What'd we just go through?

JOHN: Don't you remember? The snow and ice, the wind?

JEFF: Oh that. I slept through most of it. Nothing really...

JOHN: Nothing?

JEFF: Look, don't get on my case again this season. You're always whining about something. First it's your wrinkles, then your colour, then your lousy friends who let go.

JOHN: Well, it wasn't easy.

JEFF: Oh, give me a break!

JOHN: Okay, okay, I won't say another word.

JEFF: Good!

JOHN: Fine!

JEFF: Great!

(silence)

JOHN: Not another word.

(silence)

JOHN: If that's what you want. I won't say one more blessed thing.

(silence)

JOHN: Not even one syllable.

JEFF: Oh, for tree's sake. What is it?

JOHN: What?

JEFF: What do you want to say?

JOHN: Nothing.

JEFF: Nothing, my elbow. You've got some burr under your saddle. Might as well get it out.

JOHN: No really. I don't have anything to say.

JEFF: Fine.

JOHN: Good.

(silence)

JOHN: Except...

JEFF: Except what?

JOHN: Except, I don't know what happens next.

JEFF: What do you mean?

JOHN: Well, what do we do now?

JEFF: I can answer that. We hang on, stupid.

JOHN: We've been hanging on all year.

JEFF: So we keep on hanging on.

JOHN: Is that all there is?

JEFF: Well ... I don't know. Yeah, I guess that's about it. Hanging on. Hey, I don't know. You got a better idea?

JOHN: No, not really.

JEFF: Great.

JOHN: Fine.

(silence)

JOHN: Except...

JEFF: Except what?

JOHN: Except I thought there might be more.

JEFF: More?

JOHN: Yeah, more!

JEFF: What more?

JOHN: Well, I'm not really sure. I mean all I've ever done is hang on. It's natural enough ... but I was just wondering...

JEFF: Wondering what?

JOHN: I was just wondering what it would be like to fly.

JEFF: Fly?

JOHN: Yeah! Remember when all our buddies turned colour? They let go. Remember that?

JEFF: Yeah, poor jerks. They all let go and see where it got them.

JOHN: No, where did it get them?

JEFF: Hell! They went to hell!

JOHN: No!

JEFF: Yep, they went straight to hell. That's what happens to all leaves that let go. Didn't you see them? Went all soft inside ... starting thinking crazy thoughts. They forgot about "tight" and went limp. Tragic. Tragic. Didn't you see them let go?

JOHN: Well that's what I mean. I did see them and they were flying. I mean they didn't have to worry any more about coming loose. I watched them all go and they looked ... they looked...

JEFF: They looked scared, that's what they looked!

JOHN: I don't know.

JEFF: You "don't know?" Well, do you want to go to hell ... end up like all the rest piled deep down there? Look at them now.

JOHN: I can't!

JEFF: Don't be a wimp. Look down.

JOHN: I can't.

JEFF: Go on. Look at them down there.

JOHN: I can't, I'll fall.

JEFF: Sissy. Hang on and take a peak.

JOHN: Maybe a quick glance.

JEFF: Come on, you won't fall. I don't mind looking, and when I do, what do I see?

JOHN: I don't know. What do you see?

JEFF: A pile of nothings ... a bunch of leaves that were too chicken to hang in there when the wind blew. Nothings ... not like us real leaves. We hang in there through thick and thin.

JOHN: But, is that all there is?

JEFF: Of course it is! What else could there be?

JOHN: I just said it ... flying.

JEFF: Horse feathers. Who wants to fly when you can have it all here? Look around. Do you see anyone else on this branch?

JOHN: No.

JEFF: See anybody on the whole blasted tree for that matter?

JOHN: No ... ah ... looks like we're the only ones left.

JEFF: There, doesn't that make you feel better?

JOHN: Better?

JEFF: Yeah. We own the whole tree. We're king leaves.

JOHN: King leaves? Kings of what?

JEFF: Of the whole tree, you idiot. We rule every blasted little twig. Doesn't that put some juice in your veins and iron in your stem?

JEFF: No, I can't say that it does. I'd much rather just let it all go ... float about in the air.

JEFF: Look, you need to get with it. Stiffen up your sagging arm.

JOHN: Okay.

JEFF: Lift that drooping edge.

JOHN: Yes, sir.

JOHN: There, that's better. No more of this wimp talk. Get tight.

JOHN: Tight!

JEFF: Good.

JOHN: Fine.

(silence)

JEFF: Feel better?

JOHN: A bit.

JEFF: You have to keep hanging in there. Don't get soft or you'll end up like all the rest.

JOHN: Do you think so?

JEFF: Definitely. You're already sounding like them. Think positive.

JOHN: Positive!

JEFF: Think tight.

JOHN: Tight!

JEFF: Sing!

JOHN: Sing?

JEFF: Yeah, you remember our "Hanging in There" cheer.

JOHN: Not now.

JEFF: Sing it!

JOHN: I don't…

JEFF: You want to be a real leaf … a something?

JOHN: Yeah.

JEFF: Then sing.

JOHN: All right. Let's see, how does it go: "We only have…" Look, can't I try flying?

JEFF: Don't talk foolishness. Flying means you have to let go. That's nonsense. Now sing! It'll take your mind off flying.

JOHN: All right. (*Jeff joins in with the tune from* Songs for a Gospel People *no. 76: "We have this ministry"*)

We only have this tree
And we are not discouraged.
It is by our own power
That we can hang and swing.
In the wind and in the rain
When the branch and twigs do strain
We shall never loose our grip
Or let our fingers slip.
We only have this tree.
Our hanging is the best there is.

JOHN: That last line doesn't work.

JEFF: I kind of like it; "Our hanging is the best there is."

(*Joan, a new leaf, enters and hangs on to the branch.*)

JOAN: Hi!

33

JEFF: What?

JOHN: Who ... who are you?

JEFF: Hey, what are you doing on our tree? Who are you?

JOAN: I'm a new leaf.

JEFF: New leaf, shmoo leaf, get off this tree.

JOAN: Ah, pardon me?

JEFF: I said beat it!

JOAN: Oh dear, I don't think I can.

JEFF: Don't give me that. Just drop off!

JOAN: "Drop off?" I don't think I ... ah ... I can't.

JEFF: What do you mean you can't, you miserable little twerp? Get off this instant or I'll tear you off!

JOAN: Look. I can see that there's plenty of room here for all of us. Maybe if we all just...

JEFF: This instant, do you hear me? Let go! Now!

JOAN: I ... I can't.

JEFF: Insolence. I'll teach you a...

JOHN: Jeff ... hold off. I don't think she can move.

JEFF: Of course she can. She's just trying to get my goat. Let go right now!

JOAN: I can't.

JEFF: What...

JOAN: Please, it isn't that simple. I would if I could.

JEFF: Well, of all the...

JOHN: You look pretty new.

JOAN: Well, I just...

JEFF: Don't you go talking to her. Next thing you know, she'll be your buddy. Look, my little lady, as you can see all the other leaves have left. They were wimps ... couldn't take the wind up here and you won't be able to stand it either. I suggest you let go now and save yourself a lot of grief. Go join all the "has beens" down in hell...

JOAN: I'm not ready to...

JEFF: Now!

(Jane enters and holds on to branch.)

JANE: Hi!

JEFF: What? Not another one!

JOHN: Who are you?

JANE: I'm not sure yet. But it sure feels good.

JEFF: Not sure eh? I'll tell you. You're another little upstart. That's what you are. Get off!

JANE: Get off what?

JEFF: Get off my branch!

JANE: Put a sock in it, Jack.

JEFF: Jeff!

JANE: Jeff?

JEFF: My name's Jeff!

JANE: All right. Put a sock in it, Jeff. This branch is for everybody. If you don't like me, that's your problem.

JEFF: Well, of all the…

JOAN: I like you.

JANE: Hey, you're new too!

JOAN: Just arrived.

JANE: *(whispering)* Who are these dinosaurs?

JOAN: Don't know. They were here when I arrived.

JANE: How long do we have to put up with their guff? *(loud)* Say … how long have you been here?

JEFF: Since … ah … since … well, forever.

JOAN: That's a long time.

JEFF: It's just the way it should be.

JOHN: *(whispering)* Jeff ... we just arrived last year.

JEFF: *(whispering)* Will you shut up? If they find out we've been here for only a year, they'll want to take over. Let me handle this.

JOHN: But I don't mind if they take over. I want to fly anyway.

JEFF: Don't say that ... makes us look weak. Keep up the front. *(loud)* Yeah, we've always been here. Trainers for new leaves like you ... that us. I'm Jeff, the King of all leaves, and this is John, my ... ah ... my assistant.

JOHN: Hi.

JEFF: So if you won't leave, let's get some things straight. There are rules to being a leaf, and they're very simple.

JOAN: Rules?

JEFF: Rules. Listen carefully. Rule no. 1: "Hang on." Rule no. 2: "Don't let go." Rule no. 3: "Leaves don't fly." Rule no. 4: "I'm King of all leaves and what I say goes."

JOAN: What was rule no. 2 again?

JEFF: "Don't let go."

JOAN: Why not?

JEFF: Silly! If you let go, you'll fall off the branch.

JOAN: So?

JEFF: So if you fall off the branch, you won't be here any more.

JOAN: So?

JEFF: So you won't have any fun any more, you won't be alive, you won't be … you won't be a leaf any more.

JOAN: So?

JEFF: So if you're not a leaf, what are you?

JOHN: A bird?

JEFF: Oh, shut up, stupid! How can a leaf be a bird?

JOHN: By flying…

JEFF: Nonsense.

JANE: Why can't a leaf become a bird?

JEFF: Not you too! Didn't you hear what I said? Rule no. 3: "Leaves don't fly."

JANE: Says who?

JEFF: Says me!

JANE: Yeah, well, maybe you haven't got the corner on leaf-hood. Maybe there are other ways of looking at being a leaf.

JEFF: Nonsense.

JANE: Maybe a leaf could fly.

JEFF: Look, that's really nice, but I don't think you understand. Do try to be more practical and sensible. Leaves hang on. That's what we have always done. That's what we're doing right now. That's what we'll always do.

JANE: Why?

JEFF: Why what?

JANE: Why hang on? Why do leaves hang on?

JEFF: Because.

JANE: Because why?

JEFF: Because ... because it's right. It's fun. It's ... it's all there is.

JANE: I don't know. Maybe letting go would be fun.

JOHN: I was wondering that myself.

JEFF: Great. Now look what you've done!

JANE: I didn't do anything.

JEFF: Yes you did. You got him going again with his ideas of flying. It's hogwash, empty headed, impossible. Do you hear me?

JANE: Loud and clear. You're frightened.

JEFF: No, I'm not!

JANE: Yes you are. You don't want to let go because all you've ever done is hang on. You don't know what you'd be if you let go.

JEFF: That's not true. I know what I'd be. I'd be nothing.

39

JANE: Not necessarily.

JEFF: Look, I've had just about enough of your new ideas ... I don't have to take it. Now I'm prepared to be patient, but I won't have these new-fangled ideas rammed down my throat.

JANE: Fine. Hang there forever for all I care.

(silence)

JOAN: Nice day!

(silence)

JOHN: Not bad.

(silence)

JOAN: Isn't it great to swing in the breeze?

JOHN: Not any more.

JOAN: What do you mean?

JEFF: He means if he swings too much, he'll let go.

JANE: So?

JEFF: Don't start all over again. We watched many good friends die from a breeze just like this one today. One moment you're here, loving the life of hanging on and the next moment you're gone. Blown away. Burrhhh — sends shivers up my spine.

JANE: Jeff?

JEFF: Yes?

JANE: Were you always such an uptight imbecile?

JEFF: Humph! Just what you'd expect from a child!

JOAN: Oh, now that was mean!

JANE: He deserves it.

JOAN: Don't be so hard on him.

JOHN: It's been a long winter.

JANE: I have no patience for people who hang around and get in the way.

JOHN: He's not in the way, is he?

JANE: Sure he is. Look around. See all the new leaves coming along. Pretty soon this whole branch will be covered. We don't have space for old has-beens. Clear them out I say.

JOAN: Isn't that a bit rash?

JANE: Not at all. They had their chance to rule this branch. Make way for a new breed of leaf. That's what I say.

JOAN: But...

JANE: But nothing. Get them all off.

JOHN: I'd love to go, but...

JANE: But what?

JOHN: But I'm frightened. What if Jeff is right? What if I stop being a leaf once I let go?

JANE: So?

JOHN: So I don't want that to happen.

JOAN: I can understand. What do you want to happen?

JOHN: I don't actually know. I mean, last year when everyone else left, I remember they were frightened too. They hung on as long as they could. But when they fell … well…

JOAN: Yes?

JOHN: Well, when they fell … they looked different.

JEFF: Different. Yeah, they were rip-roaring mad that they had to leave.

JOHN: Maybe. But well, they didn't seem so anxious. I think some of them were even smiling.

JOAN: Smiling? I don't understand.

JEFF: Don't listen to him. They were scared out of their stems. The smiles were only in John's head. I've heard them scream in terror … sheer terror.

JOHN: I saw the smiles. I did.

JEFF: Well tell me, oh wise one. Why would leaves smile after they stopped being leaves?

JOHN: Because…

JEFF: Yeah?

JOHN: Because ... ah ... they were ... well ... they were free.

JEFF: Free? Hah!

JOHN: Yeah, they were free.

JEFF: Free shmee. They were scared.

JOAN: What's free?

JOHN: Free. It's ah...

JEFF: Go ahead. Tell her professor!

JOHN: Free is ... free is...

JEFF: Well?

JOHN: Free is not having to hang on so much. Free is being a leaf whether you're hanging on or falling down. Free is being able to swing in the breeze without fear. Free is floating, lifting, falling with the wind. Free is...

JEFF: Free is hog-wash.

JANE: Well put, Einstein!

JEFF: It is. Free is nonsense. It means nothing. It's a numbskull idea from a wimp that's afraid to be a leaf. Leaves hang on. That's what they do.

JANE: Why can't leaves let go?

JEFF: Because they die when they let go. Don't you hear anything?

JANE: I can't hear much with all your shouting.

JEFF: I'm not shouting!!!!! I'm a leaf and leaves hang on! Get it?!

JANE: Yeah, I get it.

JOAN: This is getting us nowhere. Let's just try to get along. It's going to be a long spring.

JEFF: Easy for you to say. You just arrived.

JOHN: Maybe I could just ... just let go.

JEFF: Don't!

JOHN: I think I might.

JEFF: No ... don't. Hang in there, kid.

JOHN: It wouldn't be that bad ... not now that I think of it. Maybe free would be fun.

JEFF: You're talking crazy ... buck up.

JOHN: Maybe I could be free once and for all. That would be so...

JEFF: No, don't start. This is how all the others went. Keep your mind on hanging on ... don't start thinking loose. Think tight. Think tight.

JOHN: Loose feels good.

JEFF: No, no. Think tight!

JOHN: "Swinging in the breeze … I'm swinging in the breeze…"

JEFF: He's going. He's going delirious. Ah … John … ah … help … ah… Oh yeah … sing! Sing it out, John: "I only have this tree…"

JOHN: "I only have this tree…"

JEFF: That's it.

JOHN: "But I don't have to stay around for ever … do I?"

JEFF: Oh no, he's out of control. Hey you! Do something! John is letting go. I can see it.

JOAN: John! John!

JOHN: Huh … what?

JOAN: John! You're letting go!

JOHN: Yeah. Ain't it wonderful?

JOAN: But you'll fall off.

JOHN: I hope so.

JOAN: But you'll die … you'll be a nothing.

JOHN: That's it. I'll be free.

JEFF: Now he's really insane. John. John, do you hear me?

JOHN: Jeff, is that you?

JEFF: John. Don't let it happen to you. Hang in there, baby. We all get these feelings now and again. Think tight ... tight...

JOHN: Oh, who needs "tight" when loose is so much fun? "I'm swinging in the wind ... I'm swinging in the wind..."

JEFF: It's too late.

JANE: Too late for what?

JEFF: You wouldn't understand.

JANE: Try me.

JEFF: Well, they all went this way ... started going soft in the head. Before you know it, they lose their grip on reality and bingo, they're gone.

JANE: John seems happy enough.

JEFF: Happy. Can't you hear him crying?

JANE: No.

JEFF: Shows how much you listen. He's desperate, beside himself with fear.

JOHN: "I'm swinging in the rain ... but now I'm happy again..."

JOAN: John! John!

JOHN: Oh, what now?

JOAN: Good luck!

JOHN: Thanks, but I don't think I'll need it. It feels good to let go...

(John lets go of the rope and starts to drift away.)

JOAN: Goodbye.

JOHN: Don't worry about me. I'm free. And you know what?

JOAN: What?

JOHN: I'm flying, and I'm still a leaf.

JEFF: Tragic!

JANE: What?

JEFF: Tragic. I've never seen anyone lose it so quickly.

JANE: What did he lose.

JEFF: His tight, his grip on it, of course. Didn't you watch him fall? He was screaming.

JANE: Screaming?

JEFF: Awful ... just awful.

JOAN: I didn't hear him scream.

JEFF: That's just because you can't understand. Never will.

JOAN: I guess not.

JEFF: I guess not.

(silence)

JEFF: Want to learn a song? It's a great little number ... keeps the spirits up and your grip tight. "We only have this tree ... and we are not discouraged... " Why don't you try?

JANE: No thanks. I have better things to do.

JEFF: Oh yeah, like what?

JANE: Dreaming...

JEFF: Dreaming?

JANE: Yeah, dreaming about flying...

JOAN: And being free.

The End.

Questions for Discussion

1. What are North Americans "tight" about?

2. Does male "tight" differ from female "tight"?

3. Is being "loose" equal to laziness?

4. Complete the following sentence. "I have the most trouble giving up..."

5. What will help you let go?

6. What does the Bible tell us to let go of? (See Matt. 5,6,7)

Chapter Three

Possession: Being and Identity

Neediness, after all, is the soil of all human feelings—of sharing, of love, of compassion, of humility, of courage. People who seek happiness by possessing themselves and by holding the resources for all their needs, who seek to eliminate their neediness are sadly closed away from their own human richness.

—McGill 1987, 85

Introduction

There was once an expert mountain climber who went off one day by himself to attempt a particularly difficult ascent of a peak set in a lonely stretch of the Alps. It was a foreboding climb, fraught with many steep inclines and perilous overhangs. In the morning the weather was fine, and the mountain climber fared well. When an afternoon storm came up from the valley, he found the path hard to follow. The hand grips became slippery and the footholds untrustworthy. During a risky manoeuvre over an imposing outcrop of granite, his nerve broke. His chilled fingers lost their hold on the cliff face, and he fell towards the valley floor many thousands of feet below.

Fortunately, he managed to grab hold of a small rope he had wedged into the rock just moments before. There he hung perilously in mid-air. Through dangling feet he watched the verdant green of the valley sway back and forth. Dizzy with fright and despairing of his hopeless situation, he cried out in anguish to the Almighty: "Help! Help! Is there anyone there?"

Silence. "Is there anyone out there?"

He cried in such a plaintive voice that soon there came a deep, resonant, and comforting reply: "Yes my son. I am with you. Trust me! Let go of the rope!"

After a pause, the man literally at the end of his rope called back, "Isn't there anyone else out there?"

We who are affluent and well endowed by the standards of the world are like that mountain climber. We can't live and let go at the same time. One seems to exclude the other. We have so identified ourselves and our own worth with having and holding that relinquishment is a frightening, unthinkable prospect. We can't let go and live.

This modern parable should shake the foundations of all North American Christian stewardship programmes. Rich people can't, won't, don't let go—not really. We hang on, cling, and possess. We own, have, and hold as if our lives depended on it. That's why we're affluent. If stewardship is a difficult concept to promote in our context, it is precisely because of this situation. As human creatures, we don't want to let go, since relinquishing seems the equivalent of dying. People will not develop into more authentic Christian stewards while this simple equation between being and having is believed.

In order to build a realistic bridge between stewardship as simple fund raising in the church and stewardship as the development of uniquely Christian lifestyles, we must understand the connection between existence and possession and ask why letting go is like dying.

Having and Being

Why do we hang on? Why do we need to possess? The first response to these questions is, using the term loosely, ontological. Stemming from the Greek word *ontos*, ontology means "having to do with the fundamental structuring of human existence." At our very essence, on the ontological plain, we human beings possess. Possessing is woven into the very fabric of who we are as creatures. Having is one of the key elements within the structure of human life itself.

Here is how possession functions as an integral aspect of human life. When we are born from our mother's womb, we are essentially "needy" creatures. In a general sense, we can say that from birth to death, human existence is a pilgrimage of need, the constant search for substance, for that which feeds our neediness on all its multifaceted levels, i.e., material, emotional, psychological, intellectual, sexual, spiritual. Therefore, possession is a natural response to the basic reality of human finitude and a healthy reaction to the vulnerability of human life.

There is no reason to be ashamed of our basic neediness. In fact, the irony seems to be that if we were less ashamed of this basic condition, we might be able to overcome it with more grace.

Most human creatures are terrified of this foundational condition of need since the undeniable message arising from our need is that we are vulnerable and essentially dependent animals. We are not God's eternal and infinite, but are limited beings living towards our final demise. That's frightening! Is it any wonder that we seek to ignore this basic condition, pretending instead that we can rise above mundane preoccupations for food, shelter, clothing, companionship. After all, they simply remind us of the inescapable finitude of human life. No one can live long with a stark awareness of neediness, and so most humans, yearning for the illusion of immortality, strive to avoid or deny our intrinsic neediness.

Therefore, we possess. In this ontological sense, possession is quite natural. We have in order to eat, and we hold in order to be protected from the natural elements. Possession can be healthy as long as human beings remain aware of the impossibility of absolute possession, are able to remember that they are basically limited, dependent creatures, and realize that no amount of possessing brings immortality.

Human sin arises, as the Bible affirms frequently, when possessing becomes an ultimate value and owning no longer serves to meet a basic need, but instead becomes a mechanism for the avoidance of our contingency as creatures, as children of God. When "having" becomes an ethic of avoidance, a way to create myself, a means of denying human limitations, then possessing is distorted and becomes a flight from healthy existence.

It is our unfortunate fate as North Americans that we live in a society that is uniquely captivated by the mechanisms of avoidance through possession. How much energy do we expend buying our way out of the unnerving reality that we too will die? A lot!

Just look around you. The entire economy, our social attitudes, and family traditions are dictated by a cycle of accelerating possessiveness. It is the dominant rationale of our cities and the *lingua franca* of our life together on this continent. Down at the shopping mall, the car lot, the department store, we "seize" bits of the world as protection against the night, against mortality. We hang signs on God's creation that read "Mine," as if we can fend off our own end through bold exaggerated claims, much like little boys in a playground who pretend they are kings of the castle.

It is not by accident that the vocabulary of possessing co-opts human discourse in our society, a world in which the cash register is our altar of sacrifice. We "have" fun. We "have" relationships. We have friends, careers. And how many discussions begin and end with things: who has the tallest, the biggest, the best? All this "having" is more than a quirk of vocabulary. Our words are carriers of cultural principles. Over-consumption is our society's response to what it knows it cannot really have— eternal life. It is an antidote to a pervasive, fundamental anxiety, the anxiety of being.

Let's face it. We have a very tenuous grasp on life and that scares us terribly. So we possess to forget and pretend that we are not frightened.

When we add to this ontological predicament the very real fact that there is a limited supply or inadequate distribution of those goods that can be possessed as protection from our basic neediness, it is not surprising that as a people and as individuals we fiercely compete in order to "have" our share. As we feel more anxious over neediness, we project our avarice onto others and climb onto the treadmill of furtive grasping, over-grasping to compensate for personal insecurity. Welcome to the world of addictive consumption!

Given the ontological roots of having and holding, the answer to the primary question of this chapter is simple. Why do human beings have trouble letting go? They do not let go because letting go is equivalent to non-being.

Situating this equation within the context of local church finance, we can understand that when church-goers place their envelope on the offering plate, they are risking non-being, albeit on a minor scale. They don't consciously debate it, but people know that each dollar donated is a dollar that will not be spent purchasing security, some small portion of protection from the sense of human neediness. And in many respects, they're right. Giving is a costly and risky business.

The equation between having and being is not complete without some mention of gender. In the present context, many people labour under what feminists have correctly identified as a masculine confusion with respect to having and letting go. Many men have misconstrued "giving" as "giving up," as capitulation or abdication. Given the ingrained either/or frame of reference that has characterized much of Western rationality (proposed and promoted mainly by male philosophers), I look upon life as an "all or nothing" proposition. If I have, I have it all. If I give up, I give up all. A little voice inside me says, "I cannot control if I do not 'have' at the same time." Moreover, "I cannot enjoy if I do not own."

While this thinking is taken for granted in many circles, it is a bit irrational. Is it not possible that this particular confusion is the fabrication of a masculine psyche? Is it not likely that the inability to let go is a product of conditioning? Do I not see life as an endless exercise in striving and achieving?

Within the masculine world as I live it, having and holding are the givens, the building blocks of all that is important. Possession is the irrefutable rule by which to live and work and by which to judge my self-worth and establish my importance *vis-à-vis* others. The point of the entire enterprise of living is to possess and increase my share of the earth's rewards. To willingly forego these dividends or to give them up is an anathema.

As I ponder relinquishment, I can feel it grating against my upbringing. I lament that I have developed the courage to achieve, but not the courage to relinquish.

Whether we are male or female, the irony of North American possessing is that in the search for freedom from neediness, we deny ourselves the very condition that is the fountain of all richness and meaning: vulnerability. Human neediness is the "the soil of all human feelings," as it is only when we sense our vulnerability, only when we reach beyond the confines of our own self-reliance, that we are touched by the love and companionship of others. When we accept our vulnerability, we are open to humility and hope. Ironically, it is only when we discover that we cannot "have" enough to overcome our own limits that we realize we are given so much. In reaching out of our neediness to others, we find our true selves.

There is another dimension to having and holding. Besides the ontological roots of possession, there are sociological reasons why we have difficulty letting go. I am referring to the link between the creation of self-identity and having.

Having and Identity

Many years ago, when I was a child of ten, I liquidated my entire estate in order to purchase glass marbles. Three dollars bought several bags. I counted them: 137. There was no greater sense of peace than knowing that I had 137 allys. I was wealthy beyond imagining, and walking around the school yard, I knew who I was. I was the kid with the most marbles—more than my friends, more than any of the girls, even more than the richest boy in the district. I was really somebody—137 marbles worth of somebody.

Linked closely to the primordial aspect of neediness is a sociological dimension of possession promoted largely by the modern consumer-oriented society. People own, not only to avoid the reality of their mortality, but also possess, in a positive sense, as a means to re-create themselves. Whether it's marbles, motorcycles, or mansions, possession has become the mirror for our individual and collective identity. We are what we have.

If this world were less structured and time bound, I would suggest you stop reading right now. Put down this book, leave all your things behind, wallets, hand bags, credit cards, keys, suitcases, cheque books, Bibles, and date books! Now go for a walk for an hour, a day! Why not spend a weekend on the streets of New York or Toronto or Chicago or Montreal? Then ask about the relationship between having and identity.

Some readers may have participated in just such an exercise or been raised in the desperation of possessionlessness. As part of a training exercise for urban ministry, I went on a weekend "plunge" designed to teach me about the ravages of poverty and homelessness. For three days I made my way in the city's core with no money, no connections or home.

Over the course of those three days, I discovered how empty I was. It was two o'clock in the morning, and I was dressed in dirty clothes, shivering on a street corner with no money, no keys or shelter, no marbles! Who was I? Left alone with myself and my rather urgent and growing sense of worthlessness, I found out what I wasn't. I wasn't respectable, so I couldn't get in to use a public washroom; I had been thrown out of two donut shops and a Howard Johnson's hotel lobby. Then, after two nights, I realized I wasn't indispensable. All the meetings, the telephone calls, the family meals were taking place without me. Stripped of my self-respect, my occupation, my car, my heavily laden book shelves, I discovered that there wasn't much left to me, not very much at all.

With moving eloquence and in his profound manner, Elie Wiesel draws the same conclusion from his experience in the concentration camps in his novel *Night*. In the dark shadows of genocide, deprived of all possessions and identifying marks, human creatures can become like animals in the night, frightened, desperate, and empty.

55

In flight from the darkness of not knowing who we are or who we are meant to be, we possess. We gather things around us because they remind us of our identity and construct for us a shimmering mirror, an illusion of what we might yet become.

In a manner similar to the equation between having and being, this sociological use of possession as a means to create identity is not necessarily wrong. After all, human beings have been dressing and housing themselves in particular ways for thousands of years. To "have" certain objects, to possess in a specific fashion, is the creative energy behind culture. Without possessions, we would be unable to create a sense of uniqueness, of distinctive, vital existence.

Unfortunately, in our present context this natural cultural energy is exaggerated or twisted. These days, a successful, possessing lifestyle is far more than a stimulus to healthy vitality. It is the operative, all-pervasive paradigm of North American identity. It is the expected norm, the goal to which we all aspire. Why else would we get in the car and drive an hour through rush hour traffic to get to the shopping mall?

Question: Who are you if you don't have a house, two and one-half children, two cars, a boat, a VCR, a television, a Nintendo machine, a home computer, and, of course, credit cards? Who are you really?

Answer: In this society, your identity is shaped by what you possess. If you don't have, you just aren't.

Why not call it the "bronze" life: self-understanding and self-worth produced and sustained by possession. Imagine our world like a gigantic tanning salon where we all attempt to capture some artificial rays, to get that nice, brown, well-travelled look. Then we're somebody! Those who live the bronze life try to shape and possess their own identity through the goods they gather. They try to sustain a pristine view of themselves, a life lived in the warm sunshine of endless summer days at the beach. Who can deny that it's an intoxicating illusion? Most of us buy into this dream to some extent.

There are several problems with the bronze life. In the first place, rather than expanding our horizons, identity generated by possession reduces the boundaries of human living. Instead of growing beyond material objects, possessors confine themselves to their possessions and the depth of living withers into "having." For example, the logic of the bronze life suggests that if one possesses a great deal, one is great. If one possesses only a little, one is nothing. Given bronze life reasoning, our capacity to laugh, love, shout, and cry, to be fully human, is governed by our ability to own. Such thinking diminishes human interaction to a paltry level, to the pathetic display of our successful "having"; it misses the point of living entirely.

A second problematic dimension of achieving identity through possession is its impossibility. Can you recall sobering moments, flashes of insight that may have come to you late on Christmas Eve? Gazing at the well-laden tree, we recognize that all the parcels in the world can never capture what we feel or speak of who we are. A mountain of presents can't tell of what is most important to us. Did you ask yourself at those quiet times if all those gifts were enough? Then did you discover that they were actually irrelevant? Perish the thought!

In our quiet moments of introspection, in fleeting wisps of self-doubt, we recognize that in spite of all the shopping sprees and bargain buying, existence is hanging by a slender thread. We all know this. After all is said and bought, we're still fragile and vulnerable beings.

We bronze folk do not like these troublesome insights and so we resolve to "have" more and more, hoping by dint of determination to achieve that illusive state of real living through real having. Identity through possession becomes, therefore, a never-ending, vicious, and frankly nonsensical circle.

Through our pathetic attempts to re-create ourselves through owning, we are like the fisher who was walking down the road to the wharf and saw a sign in the local store window that said: "All the worms you want for a dollar." The fisher went in and walked up to the sales counter, declaring, "I'll take two dollars worth."

Thirdly, the production of human identity through possession ignores the structural relationship that exists between the possessed and the dispossessed. The stark fact is that hyper-having is achieved only at the price of many others not having.

This inequality between possessor and dispossessed is most evident in the trade relationships between North and South. For example, look at the bowl of sugar on your kitchen table. It's still pretty inexpensive, right? Have you ever wondered why? The fact is that peasants on sugar plantations in Latin America are paid a pittance, a fraction of what North Americans would consider to be a just salary. Because of low wages and scarcity of land, families starve, children go uneducated, water remains contaminated, and lifespans are drastically shortened. All of this happens in order that affluent people in our culture can continue to purchase their sugar at a cheap price.

The chief ethical criticism of the bronze life is that the North American passion to re-create itself through possessing requires that millions of people go without. Poor people everywhere must be nobodies so that a very few of us can be somebodies.

The possessors know. We know, even if only intuitively, that our conspicuous consumption fosters an inequality on the basis of possession. We know this is unjust and, in guilty reaction to our knowledge, we strive to justify our actions by victimizing the dispossessed. How often have you heard: "It's their own fault. If poor people worked as hard as I do, they'd be somebody now, instead of beggars."

One has only to walk in the shoes of a welfare recipient or unemployed person to realize that to not have in a culture of possessors is like not being. You're just not valued. To be poor in North America is to be dismissed as only marginally human.

Every evening in New York's Penn Station, as in countless other public spaces across the continent, a group of homeless people gather. They sleep there by night, easily numbering a couple of hundred souls. By day, it is as if they do not exist. They are cleared away before the commuters arrive.

One woman drags a shopping trolley full of papers and bags as she is shooed from the lobby by an indifferent police officer.

Walking endlessly in a world between night and day, she rarely sleeps and can barely stay awake.

As I watch, she moves off her bench. Struggling to the coffee shop, she sits down and tries to read her paper. Just for a moment her gaze holds and then she reclines into the fold of pages and falls asleep.

The proprietor comes by and tries to move her on by shaking his keys in her face. No word of address, no human salutation. This woman is a nuisance, a biological pest to be wakened like a dog and thrown out like a hapless beast. When you don't "have" in a culture of possessors, you are nothing. You are transparent.

Once this woman had moved on to the next coffee shop, the owner sneered and proclaimed to no one in particular that "they bring it on themselves—lazy bums!" That's the ironic twist. After the economic system has taken away everything from you, your job, your home, your family, you are blamed for being dispossessed.

Given the relationship between possession and identity, it is clear why people have great difficulty letting go. Much of our self-understanding is wrapped up in holding on to what we have, in grasping tightly to all that comes within our reach. "In things do we trust"; they are our hope for self-actualization.

In response to this yearning, Dietrich Bonhoeffer's comments in one of his final letters written from prison are profound. Reflecting on the craving of the religious soul to be something special, he proposes an ethic of letting go that might redirect this culture's drive to possess existence itself. He said, "One must completely abandon any attempts to make something of oneself, whether it be a saint or a converted sinner, or a churchman, a righteous man or an unrighteous one, a sick man or a healthy one" (Bonhoeffer 1937, 193).

Such a life of letting go is a nightmare, an anomaly to the possessing bronze people. Is it any wonder that Christian stewardship leaders must expend millions of dollars persuading people to loosen their grasp on possessing if even for God's sake? Not only churches, but most social agencies confront this predicament. People won't give away what they possess because they are literally giving away who they are and the possibility of what

59

they might become. If the equation between having and identity remains unchanged, the best we can hope for is that a small trickle, a mere token of our accumulated wealth, will be siphoned off for charitable purposes.

The tragedy of the consumptive drive to find identity is that it cuts us off from the possibility of receiving so much. Think again of the camel and the needle. Now imagine a person laden with suitcases, holding them under both arms, as one does at an airport. Imagine (this won't be hard) that all the trolleys are taken. Now picture that person struggling toward the exit.

Has this person ever been you? The air is stale and somehow wrinkled, like the sweater twisted though one handle of a suitcase you can barely feel among your burdens. You're late, of course. It's hot, of course. Arriving in front of the closed door, you stand reverently waiting for the god of technology to open the gate, but the blessed electronic eye is broken. The doors remain shut, and as long as you grip your baggage tightly, you'll never be able to reach the door handle and get out.

Breaking free into human living often requires an initial letting go of non-essentials. There can be no reaching out to others, no nourishment received from others if we are not prepared to be impoverished in the process. Otherwise, one stands closed to oneself and cut off from the very interaction that brings a semblance of lasting security. Remaining captive to "things," we die. To paraphrase Jesus, in attempting to possess our life, it is lost.

In summary, I believe the pretence of ownership misses the point of being and distorts our identity. This is surely one of the central messages of the Bible's attitude towards possessions. Human beings were never meant to find lasting identify through material objects, nor can we truly find ourselves through ownership.

Possessing in this context is more complex than the above equations between having and being and possessing and identity. If we are to free ourselves to be Christians stewards, then we will have to examine the political and theological reasons why people in this context possess so much.

Experiential Learning

1. Take a day (or a couple of days if you can spare them) and live in the downtown core of a major urban centre. Take a friend for protection and companionship. Take no money. During your time on the street ask yourself these questions:

    Who am I?

    How am I treated?

    What is important to the people I meet?

    If you have the courage, you might try panhandling for change. Ask yourself how people see you. What's it like to beg? What does it do to your soul?

2. Stand in a cosmetic store or a tanning salon. What are people talking about? What seems to be important to the clients of these stores? What do the ads or posters on the walls imply about life?

3. In a group setting, have everyone take out their purse, wallet, or billfold. Examine the contents together. What do the things we carry tell us about who we are?

Questions for Discussion

1. What does the Bible say about who you are? Can you list the ways the scriptures talk about being human? (See Matt. 6:25ff.)

2. Who are you? Can you find descriptive words that do not refer to objects or possessions that define your essence?

3. What do you do when a beggar approaches you on the street? Why? What have you assumed about this person's identity?

Chapter Four

Poverty and Powerlessness

At Christmas, it gets really bad. My cheque is so small that I have to go around to churches and beg for my children. What's worse is when they don't even treat you with respect. Just 'cause I'm on welfare, they think I'm dirt—a nothing. You know, begging is soul destroying but that's what I must do to survive.

—Pam Coates (personal interview)

Introduction

It happens to me at hotel reception desks, restaurant tables, and airline counters every time I travel. I dread the question everyone asks: "Can we have you credit card number please?" Then I have to confess: "I don't have one." There's a pregnant pause, and I feel ashamed. I don't carry a credit card—not one—not even a bank card for those fancy after-hours automated tellers. Most service personnel look down at their neat pads or their eyes glaze over. I know what they're thinking: "Who is this guy? No credit cards. He must be a real loser if no one will trust him with the all-important plastic."

My not having credit cards is not a virtue on my part. In my case, credit cards are an open invitation to run up a debt I can't afford. It's true. I'm a born spender.

Each time I am asked the question, I realize again that in the industrialized world there is a connection between possessing and status and how I'm treated by others. Having the privilege to purchase, as symbolized by the credit card, is a powerful indicator of my economic importance.

It's at those moments that I understand how possessing in the North American context is a more complex phenomenon than can be explained simply by the ontological or sociological equations already outlined. If we are to free ourselves to be Christian stewards, then we will have to address the other reasons that people in our society possess so much. Let's begin by looking at the relationship between possessions and economic status and political power.

Possessions and Power

Since possession in our context confers being and identity upon the possessor, it is not a coincidence that "having" is also the basis of and pre-condition for the accumulation of power. On a strictly personal level, I define power as the capacity to control one's life choices. It seems self-evident that the more possessions you have, the more ability you have to make decisions over your life's course. Let me compare two friends to illustrate the extent to which our individual power is linked to what we possess.

Mary, a single mother with one child, lives on a fixed income. "Welfare" is what most people call it. She spends well over 50 per cent of her monthly social assistance cheque on rent and another 25 on utility, telephone, and heating costs. With the final quarter of her monthly budget, she must pay for clothing, medical supplies, transportation, and food. As Mary often says, "The only place where I have any control at all is with the grocery bill. When things go wrong and I need extra cash, the only way I can get it is to cut down on food." Consequently, there are many months when Mary eats at the soup kitchen and visits the food bank. Even the most optimistic assessment would conclude that Mary has almost no control over her life.

On the other hand, Jane also has one child, but she lives on her small salary as a teacher's aid. Life has not always been kind to her, but she now owns her own home. She spends 30 per cent of her monthly wages on housing costs, including heat and electricity. While Jane is not rolling in money, she does have enough to buy good food, provide several learning experiences for her child, and save a bit for a rainy day.

If the same emergency happens to both Mary and Jane, it is obvious who has more power. Say the fridge breaks down. Jane can choose to buy another on credit, purchase one outright, or rent one until she decides what to do. Mary has no credit. The only store in town that would sell her a fridge will offer her a 30 per cent instalment/loan plan. Since she has no cash to purchase it outright, Mary must call the welfare office for help, and Mary doesn't want to do that because then the questions will begin: Why doesn't she pester the landlord? Why can't she budget better? Does she really need a fridge that large? Doesn't she have some friends that could help out? Mary would rather not call her social worker, because "she might think I can't handle my life and then they'd take away my boy." In so many respects, Mary's life is in someone else's hands.

Jane has the power to choose, and unless she has particularly bad luck, her economic status will increase with time. Mary has very little power, and that which she has is so tenuous that an extraordinary demand on her resources will rob her of it.

As I write this chapter, I am reminded of the annual Christmas dilemma of those living on a fixed income. The festive season is never easy—loneliness and grief weigh heavily. It is, however, especially hard on those who try to scrape together a few extra dollars for presents and who subsequently fall further into debt and end up begging for charity. I once worked in an inner-city region where loan sharks took up the slack. You could buy your Christmas gifts from the back of their station wagons. A few dollars down and a few dollars a week—for many weeks, in fact.

Since no one on a fixed income can get credit, they cannot gain financial respectability. "Having," the capacity to consume, confers status.

If objects are valued as signs of real identity, and if the constant consumption of more things, either animate or inanimate, is symbolic of what human existence is all about, it follows that those in this culture who possess a good deal will be valued highly and will become powerful. Who would question that having a large bank account and an expansive estate automatically commands society's respect? Such a "significant" individual is routinely asked to sit on various decisive committees and is valued as a worthwhile member of the community.

The extrapolation is easily made: to be rich is to be right. Remember the line from Tevia's song in *Fiddler on the Roof*? Now that he is the rich man of his fantasies, he claims that people come to seek his advice "and it won't make one bit of difference if I answer right or wrong. When you're rich they think you really know." Of course, the reverse situation is also considered to be true; to be poor is to be wrong.

Is it the connection between possessions and power that transforms the issue of personal finance into a taboo subject? Have you noticed how our culture has erected a great privacy fence around individual economic practices? "No one looks in my cheque book!" You can ask me about any aspect of my life: my educational background, my family upbringing, my children's lives, my living arrangements, even my sex life, and I'll give you a reasonable response. But don't touch my salary or ask about my actual financial position. All that is my secret and my right to hide!

Given a link between wealth and power, this sensitivity is not all that peculiar. Divulging financial facts is tantamount to self-exposure, revealing what amount of power I actually possess. It is better to keep people guessing. To be open is to risk losing the power I have. It's like taking off my protective mask and divulging who I really am: a dependent and vulnerable being.

Whatever the reason for secrecy, financial stature is viewed as so important that it is written into our political and judicial structures. Those who possess are granted privilege and power. Have you seen how owning confers lawfulness on those who possess? Millionaires are not subject to the same scrutiny or moral judgements as those who are dispossessed. Great owners live in an untouchable space above the rabble, protected by the structures of our society.

The elevation of the rich is not a new phenomenon. Almost a century ago, J. S. Woodsworth, a Canadian Methodist minister and the founder of a socialist party, outlined the inequality between the possessor and the dispossessed and how the law supports ownership unequivocally. He commented upon the acquisitiveness of a coal magnate who considered that he actually "owned" the mine: "'My mine.' What a sacrilege. This little man who was born yesterday and will die tomorrow claims what it took God Almighty millions of years to provide." Woodsworth goes on to illustrate that someone who steals from the coal mine in order to give his or her family warmth is considered a thief under the law, "but in the eyes of the One who made the coal for all children, who is the thief?" (McNaught 1959, 72).

Let us leave the personal level and explore the more complex communal situation. Here as well, the dynamics of possession and power hold true. Those who own much, i.e., Northern peoples, are able to direct the lives of many in resource-based Southern countries. Such an imbalance of power is embedded in and perpetuated by current international trading arrangements. A low value is conferred on the poor countries' surplus of natural resources and a high value on manufactured goods produced in the wealthy industrial nations: we buy bananas for next to nothing while they pay exorbitantly for cars and computers.

While the current global financial structures are quite complicated, it is not false to suggest that the twentieth century draws to a close in an era of intolerable economic inequality. In part, this is because affluent North Americans find it difficult, if not unthinkable, to let go of their possessions and the power these possessions confer.

Let me introduce Alex. When he was young, he picked sugar cane for the princely sum of one dollar a day: sun rise to sun set. Cutting cane is back-breaking work, particularly if you have to load it as well as cut it. It is often also a bloody business, as the edges of the cane stalks are sharp. Alex told me how his days would begin. Every peasant had a certain section of land. When they were told to begin, all the cutters took off at a furious rate, because they knew that the quoted salary went to the first worker who finished his section. The rate dropped after that, and the last one to finish his section received nothing. Before he learned to cut quickly, Alex came home on many days with bloody hands and no money.

You may be thinking, "That's outrageous!" You're right. It is scandalous, but Alex and all the other cane cutters in plantations across the Southern hemisphere have to go home with little or nothing if we are to have cheap sugar on our morning cereal. Alex is a living parable teaching us that if we possess, we control a great deal—even the lives of unnumbered peasants in foreign lands.

Is it any wonder that people have a difficult time relinquishing their grip on the fruits of the earth? Are we surprised that many, like the Jewish ruler, go away sorrowful because they can't give it all away? No one chooses easily to relinquish status and power, to live in a state of powerlessness and, therefore, to be vulnerable to the power of others. Given that our childhood training is oriented towards striving, attaining, getting, working to have, how can we simply relinquish the power that possessing confers?

Even as we cling to the power that our possessions afford, we realize that a social order based upon this relationship between possessions and power is transient. While material goods can confer a short-term sense of control, possessing most often engenders a false coercive power that must posit its own authority through control and force in order to sustain itself.

As the Somozas and Marcos' and countless other wealthy people have discovered, the version of power achieved through possession is fleeting at best. When those who are dispossessed are no longer fooled by the illusion of omnipotence created by wealth, they will shatter the false power of the possessors. This is the law of revolution.

As the debt crisis increases, the poor nations will find it more and more distasteful to accept the imbalance of economic power structures. Why should the wealthy have it all their way? Why should rich institutions control entire nations and exact exorbitant interest charges on external debt? Why should possessions dictate lawfulness? One example of this growing tide of resentment is seen in the calls for a moratorium on foreign debt repayment in Latin America.

Fortunately or unfortunately, depending on your position, the poor nations are no longer fooled by three-piece suits and flashy commercials. Eventually the poor will claim what is their rightful share of the earth's riches.

In the next chapter, we'll examine one final reason why North Americans have difficulty relinquishing. In a society where being is equated with possessing, dispossession is not only frightening, it's immoral.

Experiential Learning

1. Draw up a list of the people who control the finances in your church. Who sits on the finance committee or the board of stewards? Why were they chosen? Are they wealthy or poor? How often is an unemployed person asked to help with church finances?

2. Do the same analysis of the local school board or the board of directors of the local hospital. Why were these people chosen? Is there some connection between status and wealth? How would you define it?

Questions for Discussion

1. How does the Bible look upon political power? Who are the powerful people in the Bible and where does their power originate? (See 1 Sam. 8:1-22). What does this say about our identification of power and wealth?

2. Can you really own anything? What do you own?

3. Is our judicial system fair, i.e., does it treat rich and poor alike?

4. What kind of power do you seek? What kind of power do you have? Is there a relationship between your power and that of the dispossessed?

Chapter Five

Poverty, Possessing, and Morality

While mission in the imperial church implies that the mission-izing community is in possession of something not enjoyed by the others (truth, salvation, righteousness etc.), stewardship in its very essence contains a polemic against the whole idea of possession, whether material or spiritual.

—Hall 1990, 134

Introduction

Whether Christians appreciate it or not, their religious tradition has forged a link between possessing and morality.

Imagine this common situation. It's Sunday morning. As worship is about to begin, a knock comes at the church door. A dirty, ragged man stands there and asks for a handout: "Have you got fifteen dollars for a bus ticket home?" His breath smells and his gait is none too sure.

What do you do? Would you give it to him? Should you give out money even if you think it might be used to purchase alcohol or cigarettes or put to some other unstated purpose? Is charity intended even for those who deceive us?

Most church-goers would consider it a terrible mismanagement of ecclesiastical funds if we gave money to someone who eventually spent it on a bottle or a smoke. To avoid such a circumstance, many schemes have been developed to ensure that charitable funds are properly spent. In order to prevent fraud, churches give out food vouchers, chits for gasoline, free food bags from the local grocer, and meal plans at the town restaurant. We tell ourselves that these mechanisms are necessary to avoid abuse. They are not meant to be demeaning or humiliating. We're just being good stewards. Isn't that what we say to ourselves?

We comfort ourselves by citing that old adage, "Beggars can't be choosers." If we're going to give out charity, then we're going to decide how it gets spent. The weakness in this argument is not evident to many of us since we have never had to beg.

Begging—I can think of no other human activity that should concern the Christian community more. To have to reach out in need, imploring benevolence from a stranger, is to be at their mercy. It is soul destroying. How often persons living on the streets have told me of their plight: "There I am with my hand out. All I need is a bit of change—a nickel, or a quarter, and everyone acts like I don't exist. They look right through me."

Surely the church must stand opposed to a circumstance, such as begging, where the human spirit is crushed. Yet when we invoke these schemes to protect our money from misuse, we often force the stranger at our door to do just that—beg for help. How ironic that the church, which springs from a homeless mother and child, can no longer see itself as one with the indigent of this day.

There are many perspectives from which to analyze the perplexing pastoral problem of giving out charity, but what we often overlook is the dubious but automatic connection made between lack of means—having to beg—and a commensurate lack of morality. If you have nothing, you are immediately suspected of immoral living habits: bad budgeting, laziness, or substance abuse.

You may well ask why this is the case. Why are possessions a sign of virtue while poverty is considered to be synonymous with immorality? The answer lies at the heart of our religious life.

In the North American context, Christians have a strong sense of God's providence. God is present in every aspect of daily life, working to bring about God's plan. It is more than a theory: the expectation of God's providential presence is as basic as the air we breathe. Under the sway of this doctrine, it is assumed that the good life, i.e., plentiful possessions, is a sign of God's blessing. Conversely, being dispossessed is a sign of God's curse.

So powerful is the link between morality and affluence that it has influenced even the cultural values of this continent. In its own way, the vast hinterland of secular society assumes that wealth is an indication of "rightness," while poverty is evidence of inappropriate or careless behaviour. In the permissive, individualistic world of the 1990s, having and holding are "winning" principles. Relinquishing is definitely "out," a losing proposition.

Leaving the secular world aside, we must look deeper than the doctrine of providence if we are to explore the concept that possessing is a theological imperative. To understand the equation between riches and righteousness, we begin with the Hebrew scriptures. Though found in other ancient writings, the link between wealth and divine favour is rooted in what is known as the "wisdom thinking" of the Bible.

Wisdom logic is simple. Wealth is God's blessing, and poverty, God's curse. It's quite a common motif. It is the basis upon which Job's comforters, for instance, interpret Job's sickness and destitution. Compressed into a couple of phrases, their message is: "Job, you've sinned somehow. That's why you're sick and bankrupt." It is against this equation that Job is forced to debate. Many religious thinkers, both before and after Bildad, Eliphaz, and Zophar, have interpreted wealth as a sign of God's favour and poverty as an indication of God's curse. This principle is also found in Proverbs (Prov. 3:9-10). In John 9:1-3, the disciples of Jesus connect a man's blindness, a curse from God, with his sin.

This logic is not confined to Judeo-Christian tradition. It may be one of the common threads running through all religious and quasi-spiritual movements. In our simple and naive way, perhaps as an antidote to anxiety or as bolster to the frightened ego, human beings have always wanted to see their possessions as tangible proof of divine favour.

In the Protestant tradition, wisdom logic has been somewhat refined and given a moral twist. The reformers, beginning with Martin Luther, assumed that God's favour cannot be gained no matter what we do or believe. Grace is a gift, and we are loved by God because of that grace. Nothing we do or say will change that. This was Luther's greatest contribution to the history of Christian thought. In light of the present discussion, his point infers that our Creator cannot be bribed by righteous works. No amount of charity, no number of pilgrimages, is sufficient to gain God's favour. Frankly, the Almighty is not interested in our guilt offerings. Not at all! Salvation? It can't be earned.

Can you imagine the impact of this idea? It was difficult for post-reformation believers to sense the radical, subverting freedom contained in Luther's thought. The twisting, torturous power of guilt was broken. The devout could believe and respond to God's action out of a liberated spirit, as did the first disciples.

As with all reform movements, it wasn't long before the second generation of recruits put their particular spin on the founder's ideas. In the case of the later reformers, this began with a question. If God's grace is a gift, then why do some receive it while others do not?

Dietrich Bonhoeffer, a member of the German confessing church in World War II, once said that no matter how hard you ask the wrong question, you'll never get the right answer. How true that is for the question of receiving or rejecting God's gift of love.

In response, John Calvin developed what he called a "terrible" idea—the doctrine of election, in which it was assumed that only some people had been chosen by God for salvation. Elected by God for this privilege, they consequently received it gladly, while others were excluded. Those excluded rejected God's offer of grace and, according to Calvin, no one knew if they were saved or not. Only God knew.

In the decades following Calvin's reforms, this uncertainty caused great concern. While it may seem a trifling matter to us, the health of one's eternal soul was not taken lightly. How does one know if one is among the company of the saved? That's a very weighty question!

Over time, some theologians came to the rescue. They suggested that even though one's state of grace was beyond knowledge, an abundant life might be the sign of God's favour, a slight indication that one lived in the light of divine love. Consequently, the notion that riches were a possible sign of divine favour led to what we now call the "Protestant work ethic."

People laboured under the great burden of wanting to know, to be certain, about their soul's salvation. This deep-seated yearning gave rise to a very rigorous lifestyle. One had to impose strict controls on one's own life to achieve signs of grace. The ascetic efforts of Protestantism are now famous. In my ancestor's homes, every pleasure was suspect. Hard work and constant labour were of value; idleness was sinful. Dancing and cards and games of chance and almost all other delightful pursuits were taboo. One's spare time was better spent reading the Bible or praying.

Such rigorous efforts produced some very wealthy people, and most looked upon their possessions as signs of God's favour. To possess was a sign of morality and clear evidence that one was working according to the providential design of God.

While he is not, strictly speaking, a theologian, one has only to read some of Benjamin Franklin's advice regarding money to understand the link made in North America between morality and the accumulation of goods.

> *Remember that time is money. He that can earn ten shillings a day by his labour and goes abroad, or sits idle one half of that day, though he spends but sixpence during his diversion of idleness, ought not to reckon that the only expense; he has really spent or rather thrown away, five shillings besides (Weber 1958, 48-49).*

Anyone, according to Franklin, who wasted time, also wasted money. Whoever wasted money was destroying one of God's creative gifts. Franklins's economic sentiments are based on his moral assumptions. Thriftiness, frugality, determination, and hard work were synonymous with moral living. These principles became the building blocks of a capitalist worldview. They have also been the stuff of Sunday school moralisms for two centuries.

Times haven't changed much since the days of Franklin. Today, money still bestows moral significance on its possessor, a seemingly virtuous state of being. We have only to listen to the hushed and reverent tones used to describe wealthy people of the church in order to sense the connection between money and morality.

The religious connection between possessions and morality is accentuated in the North American context by an individualistic focus of religious practice. When piety is understood to be only a personal affair, the tendency for possessions to be viewed as a reward for moral living is further increased. The enjoyment of the good life is God's reward for faithfulness. The relative health or sickness, wealth or poverty of the larger community has no bearing on one's affluence. There is no critical principle influencing our lifestyle. Faith is compartmentalized, detached from other worldly issues. Belief and the rewards for good living are our personal affair. So we can console ourselves, arguing that any ethical or social implications of wealth are irrelevant to the question of personal salvation.

At their roots, these exhortations of Franklin and the wisdom logic of the scriptures are founded on a religious attitude about God. Believers see the Almighty as a celestial Santa Claus, a Divine Being "who knows when you've been bad or good." For many, this image of God implicitly encourages possession as a righteous lifestyle. All too common is the assumption that God, our Creator, is really a heavenly accountant, operating with a balance-sheet model of salvation.

God of the balance sheet tallies up all the evil deeds and the moral indiscretions of each believer and places them alongside his or her noble acts and feats of faith. Then, depending on the bottom line, God attributes a blessing or curse to that person.

In Bible study, we'd call this retribution thinking. In Reformation thought, it is referred to as "faith" or "works" righteousness. No matter what its technical name, the basic logic is the same: God's love is conditional on moral behaviour, and this includes saving money and working hard.

While there are many other religious principles, this thinking is still alive in most of us. Lurking behind the loftier ideals is "let's make a deal" thinking. We would be less than honest if we didn't admit that most of us sitting in Christian pews on a North American Sunday morning pray to a "tit for tat" deity: "God, you do this for me, and I'll do that for you."

The Santa Claus image of God has always been popular. It is simple, self-serving for the powerful, and an inspiration to the poverty-stricken masses. Patterned after earthly monarchs, the calculating deity inspires rules and regulations and pays out punishment for innovation and rebellion. It's the heartbeat of Christian fundamentalism. "Keep the laws, and you will be blessed. Flaunt them, and you will be cursed." That's the reasoning. Those who are poor are simply lazy and unwilling to pay for their salvation through hard work and virtuous living. Why did Rome embrace Christianity? Certainly a major factor was this distorted image of God, which offers a spiritual rationale for social inequality. Was there another reason that Guatemalan dictator Rios Mont worshipped at an evangelical assembly every week?

Moreover, the church has found this image of God to be an effective device for the consolidation of its economic and spiritual power. The sale of indulgences by church authorities in the Middle Ages and the marketing of perpetual prayers by twentieth-century televangelists are two cases in point.

There is no freedom in this God, only a one-for-one formula of deed and consequence. There is no love—only sheer power. What has been described as the undeserved grace of God or the extravagance of divine love is missing from this *imago dei*. This God is hard-nosed and calculating. Even while we sing about grace and forgiveness, we all secretly know that everything has to be earned. There's no such thing as a spiritual free lunch; even God's love must be merited in some way. The very antithesis of an overwhelmingly bountiful God, this heavenly bookkeeper encourages a grasping, calculating faith, a "keep your nose to the grindstone" way of believing.

Given the various religious justifications for the accumulation of wealth arising from this image of God, we can appreciate why it is so difficult and distasteful for us to let go. Giving away our "stuff," unless it is done for a charitable cause, is immoral; it is a waste, almost an insult to the generosity of God. Why would I part with my money when it is my God-given reward, even right?

In the Methodist tradition relinquishment runs contrary to the theological imperative to hang on, "to earn all I can and save all I can," as John Wesley argued. (We often forget that the founder of Methodism also said "Give all you can.")

In summary, we construe a reduction in our lifestyle with a thinly veiled temptation to be lazy or an irreverence for God's gifts or a greedy spirit that wants to live solely for pleasure. Giving away all that we have may be seen as a lack of zeal in the service of God's reign and an abdication of our providentially imposed responsibility. At its heart, serious relinquishment is a denial of the retributive principle upon which our latent image of God depends.

Of course, the tragic reality is that salvation can never be purchased, nor can it emerge from a possessing mentality. God's grace breaks those who seek to grasp it through righteous living and thinking. What a hard lesson this is for religious establishments to appreciate! Wholeness, the state of grace, inner peace, eternal life, they're not for sale—ever!

Here I believe my mind misleads me. Like the rich young ruler, I turn away sadly, because when I seek to "have" eternal life, it alludes me. In a rather short-sighted fashion I believe that if it can't be possessed, it can't be enjoyed or experienced. This is indeed a tragic state of affairs, for when I accept that I am absolutely powerless with regard to "having" eternal life, I am ironically closest to being found by it.

The gospel states over and over that only as disciples abandon the secure and self-serving image of the accountant God will they encounter the scandalous extravagance of the God of grace. Only when we exhaust our attempts at possessing righteousness can we begin to live into the forgiven state where "letting go is a joyous and liberating act."

Experiential Learning

1. Go to church and observe how people talk about money during the worship service. Do you see any connections made between affluence and morality? Look at who is where. How are the wealthy treated and how are the poor regarded?

2. Watch a North American televangelist programme. What do they say about money? What do they promise you when you give a donation?

Questions for Discussion

1. Take a moment and describe your image of God. What are God's chief attributes? What does your God say about your possessions?

2. Is it evil to be idle? Why or why not?

3. Does your weekly offering to the church say anything about your faith?

Chapter Six

Letting Go: Challenges and Dangers

The accumulation of property is seen [in the Hebrew scriptures] as antisocial and luxury is linked with its human cost. Poverty and cruelty, the perversion of justice and religion, are traced to their source in an acquisitiveness that is alien to the neighbourhood principle of the covenant.

—R.B.Y. Scott et al. 1989, 85-86

Introduction

Why do believers have trouble heeding the message of the first stewardship workshop (Luke 18), that the possessing spirit is an obstacle to faithful living? It is a message reflected in the Hebrew scriptures according to the statement above by R.B.Y. Scott.

In summarizing the previous chapters, it is evident that we don't let go for many reasons. Relinquishment entails risking non-being and implies confrontation with our finitude as creatures. Moreover, to let go is to court non-identity and to be faced with our potentially empty existence. Furthermore, relinquishment of possessions implies a serious reduction in our capacity to control our own destiny. Finally, relinquishment is immoral and runs contrary to our image of God. The ethic of relinquishment requires that we redefine many of our religious definitions of salvation and righteousness, a task we have been unwilling or unable to undertake.

For all of these reasons, stewardly living based on relinquishment is not easy. It demands a profound sense of faith and courage since it involves living daily with our neediness, abandoning our individual independence, trusting in the care and mutual support of others. To live such a life free from the paradigm of "having" also forces us to let go of our personal dreams of power and prestige through possession and our illusion of self-righteousness. It implies the awesome discovery of a God whose graciousness smashes all pre-conceived notions of fairness, a God who cannot be bought or controlled.

It's time to pause, to take stock. Ask yourself, "Is letting go really necessary?" It's quite noble and prophetic to explain why letting go is difficult, but where is the evidence that it is even required? After all, it may well be the case that God intends human beings to be possessors; that our protective mechanisms as animals include the instinctive urge to grasp and hang on. Have I really any basis to argue that Christian discipleship demands "letting go"? Am I not demanding too much?

Let's hear afresh the earliest call to discipleship and weigh its costs.

Follow Me

It was a hot and sunny summer morning. Peter and his brother Andrew were repairing the family nets. It had been a long season, made all the more arduous by a lack of fish. Everyone had been searching, trying their lucky spots, dragging out their grandfather's special boat ornaments, praying to Yahweh for help. No fish! Peter and Andrew had caught not a single one all morning, and they had been up well before dawn to be the first out on the water. Not one fish to bring home to the family. Now the sun was rising high overhead and the sweat was pouring down their backs. Frustrated fingers fumbled with the twists and turns of the torn fishing net: "Blasted heat, blasted nets, blasted life!"

A lone man was walking by the shore, but Peter was wrapped up in his repair job. "Probably someone wanting fish for dinner!"

he thought. Even though the traveller stopped by his boat, Peter ignored him. "Pesky people won't leave a man alone to do his work!"

Then one of the most striking stories of the Gospels unfolds. In Mark the story is told in only three verses (Mark 1:16-18). Peter must have finally looked up or asked Jesus what he wanted. Whatever happened, Jesus asked him to be a disciple right on the spot; to drop everything and follow. And, miracle of miracles, Peter did just that.

Incredible as it seems, the Gospel writer makes a point of underlining the immediacy of Peter and his brother's response: "Straightaway they left their nets and followed him." They left their livelihood, their family position, their place in the community to become disciples. Miraculous!

The healing stories are impressive, and the parables are quite profound, but I believe the calling of the disciples is much more spectacular. Did they really know what they were giving up? Did Peter and Andrew really intend to follow Jesus for the rest of their lives? Wasn't this just a passing fancy, a dalliance for a few days?

No one can answer these questions completely. Given the post-resurrection narrative found in the fourth Gospel (John 21:3), it could be argued that all the disciples had intended to come back to fish in Galilee once the first blush of the encounter with Jesus wore off. It may have been a seasonal vocation. We don't know.

What is clear is that the initial call to discipleship inspired an immediate relinquishment. "Come, follow me." Jesus' appeal was direct and compelling, eliciting a response in kind: "Straightaway they left their nets." Not only Peter and Andrew, but James and John, Matthew, all of the disciples who are described in detail got up from their place of work and left it all behind.

Looking beyond the evidence surrounding the precise call to discipleship, we discover that there is a dimension of relinquishment in many of the encounters recorded in the Christian scriptures. "Letting go" plays a large part in the work Jesus undertakes with other gospel characters. To Nicodemous, Jesus says, "You must be born again"; from Zaccheus, "Half of what I have I give to the poor"; to the rich young ruler, "Go sell everything you have and give to the poor"; and to the lawyer who doesn't know who the neighbour is, "Go and do likewise." They are all asked to let go. To idle inquirers who would follow him, Jesus explains that those who become disciples have no pretence to ownership, no place to lay their heads. Jesus exhorts his followers to leave their family obligations behind—"let the dead bury the dead"—and abandon even their moralistic sensibilities concerning lepers, sinners, and other publicans. The path of discipleship begins with and is characterized by "letting go."

This is not a coincidence, a chance circumstance that was not intended for all Jesus' followers. The story of the sending out of the disciples, a story found in all three synoptic Gospels (Luke 9:1-6, 10:1-11; Matt. 10:1-14; Mark 6:7-12), suggests that Jesus meant his disciples to be marked by their radical poverty. The twelve are told to take no money or food. They are to be totally dependent on the hospitality of those they meet. In Matthew's version, they are not even allowed sandals or a second cloak for protection from the cold at night, nor a staff for protection against the dangers of the highway.

Disciples were possessionless travellers. Like the chosen people in the wilderness, Jesus' followers are marked by their absolute trust in God and dependence on God's care. If the biblical record is accurate, they were to be seen as the people who literally left everything behind, trusting only in their God to provide.

There are biblical scholars who argue that this dispossessed style of itinerant ministry was the initial pattern of Christian evangelism, a model set by Jesus perhaps, but certainly followed by the first bands of Jesus believers (see Bassler 1991, 56ff. for further information).

The initial reports of the church in Jerusalem found in the Acts of Apostles corroborate the idea that the followers of Jesus began their discipleship by giving away their private possessions. In Acts 2:44, we read how the earliest Christian community held "all things in common."

The lifestyle of relinquishment sounds a resonant cord in the devoutly religious. It fits with deep devotion. How else can we explain that most reform movements within the Christian tradition have harkened back to this material simplicity, to a life lived free of personal belongings? The monastic movement, one of the great reforming forces within the church that still has influence in this century, is based upon the notion that spiritual insight comes from relinquishment. Or, to state it correctly, relinquishment is a natural pre-condition of Christian discipleship. The Mennonites, Quakers, Shakers, all embraced a form of dispossessed living in devotion to God.

For all of these reasons, I don't believe relinquishment is merely a faddish spiritual technique. It is not mortification of the flesh, a pious facade or passing fashion. It is the essence of faith. "Letting go" is a natural response, perhaps *the* most natural response to the yearnings of the human heart to touch the transcendent in life.

For several years, I participated annually in what a group of friends called a "peace pilgrimage." It was a week's journey of about one hundred and fifty kilometres. The walk was a six-day seminar on the road. Visiting lecturers spoke to us about peace while we walked the miles towards our final goal. When you walk that distance you can't carry a lot of household conveniences. Living was very simple.

The lack of material encumbrances and the physical exertion of walking opened us to insights that were unattainable in a comfortable classroom. We abandoned pretence and pride as we shared our aches and pains, washed one another's feet, and lived with very few amenities. I began to understand relinquishment. There is wisdom that cannot be attained in sedentary comfort, but which is entirely understandable after a 154-kilometre march.

"Letting go" is the entry into Christian discipleship. Comfortable, wealthy Christians cannot enter the reign of God, because they can't find it. Jesus was and is right. It is easier for a Cadillac to go through a revolving door than for a rich person to enter the reign of God.

The Dangers of the Ethic of Relinquishment

I hope that I have raised many questions concerning the principles of relinquishment—the "Why would I?" and the "How can I?" sort of questions. I will address these in the following chapters.

Before we go further, it is essential that the ethic of relinquishment be qualified by some words of caution. All theologies have distortions and dangers. It is wise for us to review the pitfalls associated with the discipleship ethic of letting go.

First, relinquishment is not an ethic to be imposed upon the dispossessed. The poor, women, aboriginal peoples, and other marginalized groups have all been told by generations of white male Christians that their role in this life is to give up—give up their power, their land, their careers, their dreams for themselves, supposedly for the sake of Christ. Self-sacrifice was and is high on the list of virtues that the powerful expect of the oppressed.

The call to "give all away" should never be imposed on anyone, but it is especially unjust as an ethic for those for whom relinquishment is synonymous with living. It is an ethic for the powerful, the beginning of a theology of liberation for the oppressor. It has little to say to the oppressed.

In the second place, those who propose an ethic of relinquishment must be vigilant that it does not devolve into a twentieth-century version of traditional Christian dualism, a logic which is not so much a "letting go" of the impossibility of ownership as it is an outright disinterest in the earth. According to traditional dualism, the things that really matter, the "good stuff," are spiritual, and the flesh or "worldly" matters are either irrelevant or evil. As I mentioned above, the renunciation of material wealth and private ownership is the heartbeat of most Christian ascetic movements. But this desire can easily be reduced to outright contempt for anything to do with God's created order.

Our history as a faith is marked by the exaggerated attempts of zealous believers to rid themselves of the "things of the flesh." St. Simeon Stylites was most noteworthy in his relinquishment of bodily desires. He stayed at the top of a pillar near Antioch for twenty-one years. There were courageous monks who let go of all, including their protective clothing, and went to live in mosquito-infested swamps for months at a time. Many early Christians gave up sexual intercourse, some desert monks forswore contact with human beings of any kind, and a fourth-century circle of Roman women let go of marriage, motherhood, and bathing.

Regrettably, the distorted passion for relinquishment did not end in the apostolic age. A later example is St. Theresa of Lisieux, a medieval zealot, who was more than pleased to renounce her health, livelihood, and even life in order to follow Jesus. She waxes quite eloquently over her passion for leaving the desires of the world behind when she states:

> *From my childhood I have dreamt of martyrdom ... but I don't want to suffer just one torment.... I want to be scourged and crucified. I want to be flayed like St. Bartholemew. Like St. John, I want to be flung into boiling oil. Like St. Ignatious of Antioch, I want to be ground by the teeth of wild beasts.... With St. Agnes and St. Cecile, I want to offer my neck to the sword of the executioner, and like St. Joan of Arc, murmur the name of Jesus at the stake. My heart leaps when I think of the unheard torments Christians will suffer in the reign of the anti-Christ. I want to endure them all (Hall 1986, 175).*

Unfortunately, this perverted dualism did not die with the Enlightenment. On this continent, it lives on in fundamentalist doctrines like the premillennial return of Jesus: a theory that argues that the earth must be mostly destroyed before God's reign arrives. Since the earth is of so little account, its loss is a small price to pay for the rapture of eternal life. In keeping with this right-wing theology, many Christian believers have abandoned all interest in the continuance of earthly existence and concentrate instead on their spiritual salvation.

I believe such dualism runs contrary to the prophetic dimensions of Christ's mission to feed the hungry, heal the sick, and invite marginalized persons into the community of God. It is a perversion of the call to discipleship and antithetical to the spirit of the gospel. I feel so strongly about the Bible's primary concern for the health of the created order that I believe any doctrine that leads people to abandon the earth prematurely is unchristian.

Contrary to a perverted dualism that discourages any concern for discourse with creation, relinquishment allows us to cherish the earth in all its fullness. We may decide not to possess, but this does not mean we should cease to relish the fruits of God's creation or revel in the mystery of bodily existence or exalt in the beauty of God's world. Rather, we who seek to possess nothing are free to enjoy all the delights of existence. Relinquishment, while it has some superficial similarities with earth-denying dualism, must guard against that temptation.

One last, and perhaps most important, note of caution: Relinquishment is not blind abdication. I know there is a tendency within me to decide that if I can't own or "have" something in its entirety, then I don't want any part of it. Most recently, I have sensed this logic operative in debates over our role as creatures within a deteriorating ecosystem. Whereas classical dualism suggests that the earth and its health are irrelevant, a new voice proclaims that human attempts to correct past errors are presumptuous and misguided.

I hear echoes of what we might call an "abdicationist" point of view lurking behind seemingly "progressive" arguments about the failed human experiment, as if it is pointless for humans to assume any managerial role in the restoration of the planet. It's all or nothing. "Away with false hierarchy and human presumption of importance. We have ruined the globe, let's not assume we are the only ones who can fix it. Let the insects take it over." Admittedly this is an exaggeration, but the temptation of total renunciation does sometimes hide behind even the most virtuous statements concerning the human place in the revitalization of the earth.

I understand the frustration that might lead to abdication, but in a more critical sense, this all or nothing attitude is an unfortunate product of the Western either/or frame of reasoning. That is often our way. We suffer ambiguity poorly, and our souls do not bend easily. True relinquishment will require our greatest efforts at this point: tolerating the greyness, embracing a both/and approach to living.

Our role as Christian disciples must be to discover some middle ground between absolute control and total abandonment. It is at this point that the biblical symbol of the steward is helpful. Relinquishment, when it is attached to a dialectical concept such as the steward, offers some inspiration. We are called on to relinquish our possessive spirit, but in so doing we are not relieved of our responsibility to care for creation.

Experiential Learning

1. Do a survey of the men and women within your circle of friends and ask them if they would be willing to give up their careers. What event, object, or idea would tempt them to make such a choice?

2. Take time to visit a monastic community. Try to enter into the spirit of their communal life. Ask yourself what its central purpose might be and where its spiritual depth originates.

Questions for Discussion

1. Divide the discussion group into men and women. Ask each group to answer the following questions and then compare responses.

    (a) Who has power in our society? Who is asked to relinquish?

(b) What do I possess that I should relinquish? How should I let
go?

(c) Does the Bible call upon men and women to let go in
different ways? Do you agree with the scriptures?

2. What did Paul mean when he said that Christians should
"adapt themselves no longer to the pattern of this present
world... "? (Rom. 12:12).

Chapter Seven

Standing By to Standing With

Unless we are willing to stand with the oppressed by first breaking our attachment to wealth and comfort, all our talk of justice will be sheer hypocrisy.

—Wallis 1984, 66-67

Introduction

Why would we relinquish anything? Why would we give away one blessed thing? When we feel guilty, we'll donate to a needy cause, but that's not real relinquishment. We still keep a pretty close rein on our "stuff." For all of the reasons already cited, any rational person would hang on for dear life. Many North Americans do just that. Why should Christians be any different? This chapter begins to explore that question.

Again, it's time for play. We often labour under the false assumption that learning, if it is to be "good" and "solid" and "rigorous" and "serious," must also be arduous and boring. Not so! Real education is usually engaging and exciting. Here's your chance. I want you to call some friends together and act out the following play. You can each take a part to read. If you have more energy, you might try adding some actions to the words. Whatever you do, I think you will find it entertaining and revealing. It will begin to shed some light on why and how relinquishment might be an ethic for the powerful.

Three people are hanging onto a branch, stick, or rope, symbolizing leaves hanging from a tree. It is early summer.

JEFF: So…

JANE: Huh? What?

JEFF: So…

JANE: So? So what?

JEFF: So are you ready to talk now? So are you ready to stop your dreaming and be decent leaves?

JOAN: *(yawning)* Huh? What's that?

JEFF: Oh, you're awake now too? I said maybe you two could stop your senseless dreaming and get on with being good, conscientious leaves.

JOAN: Oh, what do you mean? How do I become a good consc … conscut … conscience … *(yawning)* whatever you said.

JANE: Wake up! He means talking leaves again.

JEFF: Right!

JANE: He means leaves that don't dream.

JEFF: Correct.

JANE: He means leaves that listen to his long-winded sermons about "tight."

JEFF: Just so ... er ... except the part about long winded. "Tight" is important. It's the essence of leafness. Without tight we are nothing, mere victims of circumstance. It is time that you two learned about standing by the strength of your tight.

JANE: See what I mean?

JEFF: Are you two listening to me? Tight is the primary building block of our ontological structure. It allows us to stand tall and proud.

JOAN: Oh dear.

JEFF: ...the chief attribute of all life in which leaves take part.

JOAN: *(whispering)* Must we listen to this all over again?

JEFF: ...the goal towards which leafhood is constantly becoming.

JOAN: I was having such a good time *(yawns)* dreaming.

JANE: Me too, maybe we can shut him up if we humour him a bit.

JEFF: Tight is the power which moves all things, it is ... it is ... all in all.

JANE: Hey, Jeff.

JEFF: Huh? What? You have a question?

JANE: Yeah.

JEFF: Very good, you're actually catching on. Go ahead.

JANE: Why tight?

JEFF: What do you mean, "Why tight"? There is no other. Tight is right.

JANE: But why not "loose"?

JEFF: Silly, loose is the antithesis of all that is. It is anti-tight, contrary to the ground of all tightness.

JANE: But I like loose.

JEFF: Heathen! Nincompoop! It's wrong. It undermines and subverts everything leafhood stands for.

JANE: But loose feels so good.

JEFF: Of course it feels good. That's the problem. Tight is better because it hurts so much.

JOAN: Hurts?

JEFF: Hurts. When something hurts it must be good, because it draws us into the great tightness of all things. Without hurt, tightness would be meaningless; without meaning, leafhood could not stand.

JANE: What if the essence of all things is looseness?

JEFF: Nonsense! You don't even know what you're talking about.

JANE: Why not? Why not looseness?

JEFF: This is sheer rubbish.

JANE: Looseness feels good. It must be best!

JOAN: I'll go for that. Looseness is all in all. I think I heard a song about that once. Ah, "Thine is the looseness..."

JEFF: I'm not listening to this any longer. It's, it's ... heresy.

JANE: See?

JOAN: It worked.

JANE: Shuts him up every time.

JOAN: Sure does.

JANE: Old fool. Wouldn't recognize his own feelings if he fell over them.

JOAN: Too bad.

JANE: I don't feel sorry for him. He's had his time. It's not our fault if he's wasted it on his "tightness."

JOAN: Yeah. I suppose so.

JANE: Well...

JOAN: That's that.

JANE: So ... ah ... well...

JOAN: Yeah?

JANE: Nice day.

JOAN: Sure is.

(silence)

JOAN: What about…

JANE: What about what?

JOAN: Well, I was just wondering. I mean, why…

JANE: Why what?

JOAN: Just … just why are we here?

JANE: Well, to dream, to dream about flying.

JOAN: I like that.

(silence)

JOAN: Is that all?

JANE: Well, I suppose…

JOAN: Yes?

JANE: I suppose we are meant to swing in the breeze.

JOAN: I like that too, but … is that all there is?

JANE: I'm not sure. There's … er … there's looseness.

JOAN: Looseness?

JANE: Yeah. We're here to embody looseness, to give glory to the great looseness that binds all that is.

JOAN: Now you sound like Jeff.

JEFF: Huh? You called?

JANE: Go back to tight, old man.

JEFF: Humph. Just like children. Insolent little things.

JOAN: What's so great and important about looseness?

JANE: Well, it feels good.

JOAN: Yeah, so?

JANE: Well, it's better than tight.

JOAN: So?

JANE: So...

JOAN: So?

JANE: So ... so I don't really know why we're here. What do you think?

JOAN: Well, maybe we're here for something else. Maybe we don't just stand by and watch things happen all around us. Maybe we're here to stand ... to stand with something greater.

JANE: Greater than loose or tight?

JOAN: Yeah.

JANE: Like what?

JOAN: I don't know ... ah ... maybe we're supposed to do something while we're here.

JANE: Do what?

JOAN: I don't know. But I was wondering…

JANE: Yeah?

JOAN: See that bright ball up there?

JANE: Where?

JOAN: Over there. Turn around. You can see it over behind the tree just now.

JANE: Oh yeah, I see it.

JOAN: It moves.

JANE: I know that!

JOAN: Well, maybe we're supposed to do something with that ball.

JANE: Like what?

JOAN: I'm not sure.

JANE: Oh.

JOAN: Maybe it has to do with the hot-cool feeling I get.

JOAN: Hot-cool … say, I've had that too.

JANE: Sometimes my shiny side gets so hot…

JOAN: You too? That's amazing!

JANE: And my ribbed and dull side stays cool.

JOAN: Hey, that's what happens to me! I can't believe this.

JANE: Do you think it happens to every leaf?

JOAN: I don't know. Let's ask Jeff.

JANE: Are you sure?

JOAN: It can't hurt. He might know something about hot and cool.

JANE: Hey, Jeff!

JEFF: Humph.

JANE: Jeff?

JEFF: (*yawns*)

JANE: Jeff. Wake up!

JEFF: I'm not sleeping!

JANE: Good. Listen do you know anything about...

JEFF: Hot and cool?

JANE: You were leavesdropping.

JEFF: No, I wasn't.

JANE: You were so.

JEFF: Was not!

JOAN: Oh, for tree's sake. Stop it you two.

JEFF: She started it.

JANE: I did not.

JEFF: I wasn't leavesdropping. I was trying not to listen, but being stuck on the same branch as two blithering idiots, I can hardly not hear what you're saying some times. Even if it is nonsense.

JANE: All right, what about hot and cool? Have you ever noticed how...

JEFF: How the shiny side is hot and the ribbed side is cool? Sure I have. We debated that all last summer and came to the conclusion that it means nothing. Nothing at all.

JOAN: What do you mean, nothing?

JEFF: Well it has no bearing on being a leaf, not really. Tight is the only significant factor. When you lose tight, you fall off the branch. What could be more fundamental than that?

JANE: Being hot?

JEFF: Silly girl. What has hot got to do with being a leaf?

JANE: Well, it's ... it's ... I don't know.

JEFF: Just as I thought. While you're at it, haven't you noticed yet that it changes?

JOAN: Changes?

JEFF: Changes. When that big ball is over there *(pointing to horizon)* we're all pretty cool. When the shiny ball moves overhead, say there *(pointing to high noon)*, we get hot, and then when it moves again to over there and disappears, we get really cool.

JANE: Hey, you're right!

JEFF: Sometimes I can be.

JOAN: But what does it mean?

JEFF: Nothing. It means nothing.

JANE: Nothing?

JEFF: Look, I've been here a long time and been a part of many long debates about leafhood, and we have looked at it from every angle but down. Hot and cool mean nothing.

JOAN: That's it!

JEFF: What's it?

JOAN: "…from every angle but down." That's it.

JEFF: What are you talking about?

JANE: Yeah, what are you talking about?

JOAN: What about from down there? Maybe hot and cool make a difference down there.

JEFF: Nonsense.

99

JANE: What could our hot and cool have to do with down there?

JOAN: Well, maybe ... you know, how when we're hot on one side...

JEFF: Yes, it's still cool on the other. So?

JOAN: So maybe it gets cool down there too? I mean maybe we keep the hot from down there.

JEFF: But there's nothing down there.

JOAN: Nothing?

JEFF: There's nothing down there. It's hell. It's where we all go if we lose our tight.

JOAN: But maybe there is something ... something that needs to stay cool. I mean, I saw our friend ... what was his name?

JEFF: John.

JOAN: Yeah, I saw John go down there. He looked happy.

JEFF: He was terrified, but what does it matter. He's a nothing now.

JOAN: But what if he isn't?

JEFF: Isn't what?

JANE: A nothing. What if he isn't a nothing?

JOAN: Then we would be keeping him cool.

JEFF: This is crazy.

JOAN: No, it's not. Think about it. We might have a purpose, something greater than tight and loose. We might be here to keep the hot away.

JEFF: You're talking foolishness.

JANE: I like that. Keeping off the hot. I could live for that.

JANE: Makes me feel a bit better.

JEFF: You're both nuts.

JANE: Oh, loosen up Jeff, and think a bit.

JEFF: I am thinking.

JANE: Then you must be able to see that Joan's idea does have a certain … a certain logic about it.

JEFF: Logic smoggic…

JANE: Think about it though. We're here to keep the hot off down there.

JEFF: Well…

JANE: What do you think?

JEFF: Well … all right, all right. She's got a point. I grant you that. It's a very good, I mean a very intriguing theory, but … but that's all it is. A theory.

JOAN: But what if we went down there to find out?

JEFF: Great idea.

JOAN: Yes. I would just drop off and find out and then...

JEFF: And then you'd fly right back up and tell us?

JOAN: Yes, I'd fly right... Say, I couldn't fly back here, could I?

Jane: It was a nice thought.

JOAN: But...

JANE: We'll just have to leave it as a good theory.

JOAN: But it might be true. We might have a purpose after all.

JANE: I'd like to believe you kid, I think I do, but we'll just have to let it go at that.

JOAN: At what?

JANE: At belief.

JEFF: At a nice unsubstantiated theory.

JOAN: Oh. I was hoping...

JANE: Hoping?

JOAN: Hoping for more. Something real...

JEFF: Nice idea. Really nice idea.

JOAN: Maybe I'll let go and find out.

JEFF: Don't be silly. Leaves don't let go.

JOAN: But then I would know.

JEFF: But we wouldn't, would we? What good would it do for you to find out if the rest of us don't hear about it?

JOAN: At least I would know I was right.

JEFF: Great, just great. "Drop off!" "Go down!" What are leaves coming to these days? No spunk, no courage, no tight! Leaves hang on.

JOAN: But...

JEFF: But nothing.

JANE: I admire your courage, but would you really let go just to prove a theory? We enjoy your company here.

JOAN: But I would know.

JANE: Can we ever really know?

JOAN: I want to ... ouch!

JANE: What?

JOAN: Ow! That hurt!

JEFF: What's the matter?

JOAN: Did you do that?

JEFF: Do what?

JOAN: That little sting. Did you prick me with your stem?

JEFF: Of course not.

JOAN: Ouch! There it is again.

JANE: Joan, are you all right?

JOAN: I don't know. Didn't you feel that?

JANE: Feel what?

JOAN: The little ... ow! ... the pinch near my stem.

JANE: I didn't feel a ... ouch!

JEFF: You too? What's the matter?

JANE: I don't ... ow! ... know.

JOAN: It's like a ... a hot pinch.

JANE: That's it. It comes on all of a sudden and then slowly slides away.

JEFF: Slowly slides away?

JOAN: That's right.

JEFF: Turn around!

JOAN: What?

JEFF: Turn around, I say.

JOAN: Why...

JEFF: Just do as I say. This instant.

JOAN: All right, you don't have to get snarky. *(she turns)*

JEFF: You too. *(speaking to Jane)*

JANE: Why should I?

JEFF: Do it and don't argue.

JANE: Okay, okay. If it'll make you feel better. *(she turns)*

JEFF: Uh oh!

JANE: Uh oh, what?

JOAN: What's the matter?

JEFF: Hmmn. Looks like tight eaters.

JANE: Tight eaters?

JEFF: Tight eaters.

Joan: What's a tight eater?

JEFF: I don't know exactly.

JANE: Great. He doesn't know "exactly."

JEFF: Listen, I've only heard about them. Some old leaves that I met when I arrived last year told me of a legend, a story, about a thing that comes to the branch. Who knows when and who knows why? But they come and they eat away at your tight, right down by the stem, until you ... until you let go!

JANE: Did they ever see one of these ... ouch! ... things?

JEFF: One really old guy said they looked like little leaves curled. All green, with no stem. Ugh. Makes me sick just to think about it.

JANE: Little leaves all curled up…

JANE: Eating away at the stem?

JEFF: It's sounds awful and incredible, I know. But that's how the legend goes.

JANE: Ow! Well…

JEFF: Well, what?

JANE: Well, can you see anything?

JEFF: Ah… *(looking closely).* Nope. Nothing.

JANE: Are you sure?

JEFF: Sure. Nothing at all.

JANE: Then why did you tell us the story?

JEFF: It's nothing. Don't think about it. Really. It's just an old leave's tale.

JANE: Jeff, you're lying. Tell me the truth. Are there little green things at my stem?

JEFF: Ah…

JANE: How about me?

JEFF: Well, there's only a few. Probably nothing.

JANE: Do they look ... ouch! ... like little tight-rolled leaves?

JEFF: A bit, yeah, but I'm sure it's nothing. Really!

JOAN: Ouch! That's beginning to hurt. How about me? Do you see any of those things on my stem?

JEFF: Well ... ah ... yes, there are a few there too.

JANE: Great. What do we do now?

JEFF: I, ah...

JANE: What does the legend say? Is there any way to get these ... ouch! ... these things off?

JEFF: Not much.

JOAN: Ow! Isn't there anything at all we can do?

JEFF: They did say one thing. This old guy said that if you make a lot of noise, the tight eaters will come to you first ... you know, swing around a lot. They seem to like the motion or something.

JANE: What good does that do us? They're already here. And besides, we don't want to attract them, we want to get rid of them.

JEFF: Well, maybe if you stand still. That's it. Stand still. They might go away and look for a leaf that is moving.

JANE: Still?

JEFF: Still. Don't say a word.

JOAN: All right.

JANE: Maybe it will work.

JEFF: Still!

(silence)

JANE: But...

JEFF: Shhhhhh!

JOAN: Mummumumumum!

JEFF: Still! Be still!

JOAN: Ow! I can't!

JEFF: You can't what?

JOAN: I can't be still while these things are hurting me there!

JEFF: Try.

JOAN: All right...

(silence)

JANE: Ow! It's not working. They're still here.

JEFF: Well, that's all I know.

JANE: Great. Big help you are.

JEFF: Look, it's not my problem. You're the ones who have the tight eaters. I'm just standing here beside you.

They're not on me. Solve it yourself.

JANE: Say, that's right. How come they don't go after you?

JEFF: Don't know. I suppose you're more interesting, new and green and all that.

JOAN: Can't you think of anything?

JEFF: I'm sorry, I've done all I can.

JOAN: Ow!

JANE: Ouch! Oh, this is getting unbearable!

JOAN: Can't we ... ow! ... can't we do anything?

JANE: Ouch! Just hang in there...

JOAN: Oh, oh, oh, it's getting harder to hang on. Ow!

JANE: Ouch! Jeff, please. Isn't there anything you can do?

JEFF: I'm not involved. It's nothing personal, but this isn't my issue ... not really.

JANE: Please.

JOAN: Can't you think of anything?

JEFF: Don't bother me. I'm trying to stand still.

JANE: A big help you are. Ow! A real friend.

JOAN: Oh, leave him alone. He doesn't care about us.

JANE: You're … ouch! … right.

JOAN: If only I could shake them off!

JANE: Ow! Maybe we could try.

JOAN: Let's see … ouch! It's not such a nice feeling now. I feel like I might let go … ouch! … if I shake too hard.

JANE: Let me try. Ow! It hurts even more.

JEFF: Don't shake—it makes things worse.

JANE: Oh, leave us alone.

JEFF: I'd like to, I really would, but you two are disturbing me. I can't stand still, and I'm afraid the tight eaters might spread all over this branch.

JANE: Well, do something then!

JOAN: Please … ow! … please, before it's too late.

JEFF: Well…

JANE: Ouch! Ow! Oh, help!

JOAN: Help! Please…

JEFF: All right, all right! I never thought it would come to this.

JANE: What … what are you doing?

JEFF: Shaking, stupid. Can't you see?

JOAN: Why?

JEFF: Just stand still and keep quiet.

JANE: Jeff, if you shake, they'll start to come on your stem too.

JEFF: Stand still, will you, and don't say anything.

(silence)

JEFF: Come on, come on... Maybe if I do a little dance. Hey, little tight eaters, come on over here. Don't stay with those little ones. Why not try a big old leaf? Bet you can't bite my stem. Come on...

JANE: Jeff!

JEFF: Just shut up, will you? Come on, come on, little tight eaters. I bet you can't eat through my stem. I bet you're afraid. Come on, come on...

JANE: Hey...

JOAN: Oh...

JEFF: Keep coming, you little good for nothings.

JANE: Hey, they're leaving my stem. Jeff, they're leaving my stem!

JEFF: Will you be quiet? Stand straight. Let me do the swinging. Come to me... Say, do you little things like music? How about a song? "We only have this ... ow! ... tree. And we are not discouraged. Ow! It is by our own power ... oh!" Come on little tight biters, you can't trick me. I'm king of the tree...

JOAN: Oh, that's feeling better.

JANE: They're almost gone from my stem.

JEFF: Just … ow! … just don't move. Let's try a watoossee. There you are. That's some dance step for an old geezer like me. Everyone on board. Ouch! Don't miss your turn to take a bite out of the oldest stem on the tree. This it is the best stem around. Ouch! Ow! It hurts. Come on…

JOAN: They're all gone off my stem.

JANE: Me too, me too. Jeff, they're all going to you.

JEFF: Good. Have I got them all?

JOAN: I can't see.

JEFF: "We only have this tree. Ouch! I'll turn around. *(he turns)* What do you think?

JOAN: Your stem is covered. Oh, Jeff, stop your swinging! You might fall off!

JEFF: Jane, see any more on the branch?

JANE: They're all on you now. Jeff, what are doing? You'll swing right off if you're not careful. What are you doing?

JEFF: Trying to keep them all on my stem.

JANE: Why?

JEFF: Why, what?

JANE: Why are you doing this?

JEFF: Maybe I'm … ouch! … tired.

JANE: Tired of what?

JEFF: Tired of just standing by. Tired of not caring. Tired of doing nothing, nothing but hanging on. Are they all on me still?

JANE: Looks like it.

JEFF: Good. Ouch! Ow! Now for the fun part.

JOAN: What are you going to do now?

JEFF: Let go!

JOAN: Let go?

JEFF: That's right. If I can just stretch a bit to this side...

JANE: Hey, wait a minute. You're always the one who said to hang on!

JEFF: Yeah.

JANE: Well, now you're going to let go.

JEFF: I'm going to try. If ... ouch! ... if I could just...

JANE: What about all that business about "tight," about "leaves being leaves because they hang on"?

JEFF: Maybe that's not all.

JOAN: You mean...

JEFF: Maybe leaves have to do more than just hang there, just stand by and watch things happen. Maybe we have

113

some other purpose, like standing with someone... *(he drops off)*

JOAN: Jeff, you're falling!

JEFF: I know that, numbskull. Here goes.

JANE: He took all the tight eaters with him.

JOAN: Jeff, about the hot and cool. Pretty soon you'll know if I'm right, if leaves have a purpose.

JEFF: Yeah, I guess I will. Hey, Jane?

JANE: Yeah?

JEFF: I'm flying!

JANE: Why'd he do that?

JOAN: Do what?

JANE: Take all those things with him and just drop off?

JOAN: He wanted to know about down there, about the purpose for being.

JANE: Maybe. You know what I think?

JOAN: What?

JANE: I think he just wanted to be a hero, a big hero, and show us once and for all he was king.

JOAN: Maybe. You have to admit though, he finally let go.

JANE: Sure did.

The End.

Questions for Discussion

1. What are the circumstances in which you would be willing to sacrifice your life for another?

2. Have you ever been part of a poor community, a company of people who were dispossessed? What did it feel like? What did you want richer, more powerful people to do?

3. Are there ways in which the powerful can let go that will help the powerless? Should the powerful always let go?

Chapter Eight

The Action of Solidarity:
The First Step in Stewardship Lifestyles

*What the rich are being called upon to relinquish is in fact not
their possessions, but merely that which they have either naively
or wilfully withheld from their brothers and sisters for whom
they are mere trustees—and what now scandalizes their relationship with both God and neighbour.*

—Murphy 1985, 178

Introduction

So how do we do it, give it all away? This is both a spiritual and a
practical question. We'll leave the practical side for the next
chapter and address the spiritual dimension here.

How do people let go when their very being, their sociological
training, their political common sense, and their religious upbringing teaches them to hang on?

When we examine the question of relinquishment from the
point of view of the offering plate, it is more and more evident
that the present generation of church attenders give in a short-
term fashion. We will give as long as we receive something in
return: a tax receipt or a word of gratitude. Giving has devolved
into a matter of exchange, and the Sunday morning envelope is a
liturgical tool for the gifting exchange to take place.

116

In past generations, giving meant letting go of our control over our resources. There is currently an unwillingness to trust in the wisdom or authority of others. We want to get something for our gift and we're not always sure that our churches or other agencies will get it for us. In addition, the long-standing loyalty to the organization that was typical of the past is more difficult to engender in present-day believers. Fewer members truly relinquish.

The challenge of discipleship is to break the mentality of exchange, the logic that informs most philanthropic enterprises. How do we give without expectation of return? The gospel message is unequivocal: Christian discipleship begins with a genuine relinquishment, something beyond charity.

For this reason, I believe stewardly discipleship in North America must begin with a programme to promote the principle of self-relinquishment combined with a critical study of the mentality of ownership that rules our society's approach to material objects. Finally, an analysis of the economic structures that encourage covetousness on the part of the powerful is in order. Until these subjects are taken seriously in church and seminary alike, stewardship on this continent will be a feeble exhortation to give of our excess for the deserving poor.

Are you feeling uncomfortable? I've been talking about the "shoulds" of relinquishment for seven chapters. If you're like me, you'll be looking around the living room at all the material things you've gathered and feeling bad, accused, and guilty. You're saying to yourself, "Well, all right. Maybe I do have too much. Maybe I should do something. Maybe I should give something away. Maybe I should get rid of the boxes of shoes in the garage and the unused clothes in the basement. Maybe I should, maybe I should."

Let's abandon this line of thinking and relax our guilt reflex a bit. Relinquishment is not something that most of us can achieve on our own. It is one of the most difficult truths to incarnate in our own lives with honesty and a free spirit. If we start from personal guilt, we usually end up at a dead end—berating ourselves for being unfaithful and cowardly. Stop and remember that none of the disciples were perfect. They argued over who would have the best seat once the reign of God arrived. They vied for prestige. Jesus had to constantly remind them of their mission. For that matter, there are very few biblical characters, judges, prophets, or kings who make a virtue of their poverty.

We have to realize that relinquishing is not redemptive. All too often ascetic movements forget this fact. Letting go has no intrinsic value or spiritual merit. Rather, it is a pre-condition, preparing us to be recognized by and received by God's forgiving presence.

In the final analysis, just talking about relinquishment is pointless, if not counter-productive. The life of letting go begins with an encounter with a living God, a second conversion. Like the first, this conversion is experienced as a spiritual, emotional, and intellectual turning about. It brings in its wake the turmoil, zealous energy, and drastic shifts in thought and deed that are often signs of one's first encounter with God.

Relinquishment conversion is simultaneously a confrontation with a God who loves and a decision to live differently. This leads to an act or more likely a series of acts of gradually letting go. It is an anxious, yet strangely relieved peace of both the mind and heart, which have been liberated from the grasping predisposition of our acquisitive world.

Like all conversions, the relinquishment conversion may occur in different ways for different people. For some, it comes like a lightning bolt; to others, it may be a periodic challenge; and to others still, it may come as a natural evolution of faith. Whatever our response, I believe this conversion begins with a particular encounter with the God revealed in the cross.

The primacy of this encounter is explained in what I consider to be the second stewardship workshop, described in Matthew 25:31-45. After a description of that event, I will offer some tentative remarks about the conversion of the spirit, which is central to the relinquishment conversion.

Workshop Two: The Unknown Encounter

Jesus has taken his travelling lecture series to the very heart of the Jewish religious establishment—the temple mount. There he confronts the authorities on matters of the law, the prophets, the Romans, the messiah and religious authority.

In one dramatic turn after another, he undermines the reigning wisdom of his day and proposes a radically different vision of the religious quest and the faithful community. To a crowd hungry for deliverance from Roman oppression and taxes, he counsels careful watchfulness and patience. To the self-righteous, who expect to be included in the messianic feast, he promises exclusion. To the devious, he offers vulnerable innocence.

From the reaction of his disciples, it is evident that many of his words miss their mark, at least initially. It is as if he were speaking another language. The friends of Jesus had come into the Holy City dazzled by the splendour of Jerusalem and feverish with the expectation of Christ's immanent rule as messiah. As the debate drones on, I picture them becoming more uncertain and confused, scratching their heads, and hopping from one foot to the other like impatient school boys wanting to get outside to play.

Many of the early band of followers had heeded the message of the first workshop. Here they were, without money or house or employment. They had done as Christ had asked. Can you imagine the courage they had? Not understanding the implications of their actions, they had given up their nets, their homes, changing tables, families, and friends. Oh yes, they grumbled and harboured gilded expectations of wealth and the glory to come. Yet, they had taken that first step. It was not easy nor was it entirely complete and absolute. Nevertheless, they had relinquished much because of their encounter with this mysterious carpenter-preacher.

As they walked through the gate on that first evening of the Passover festival week, away from what they had anticipated would be the firing shot for the great revolution, they must have been dismayed, perhaps even angry. "Is that all? Is that all Jesus is going to say? What about overthrowing the filthy Roman oppressors? What about re-establishing the Davidic monarchy? What about armies sweeping down with the strength of God's mighty arm? Did we give up everything for this, esoteric debates in the temple?"

Once at the Mount of Olives, I imagine the disciples approaching Jesus, timidly, of course. No one wants to appear ignorant or ungrateful. Maybe it was Peter who spoke first. Matthew doesn't stipulate. "So ... ah ... when is your reign going to start, master?" There is a general murmur of agreement. This is a good question. The crowd of followers gathers round to hear how Jesus will respond.

Any reader who can remember the wonder and urgency of adolescence will recognize this style of question. I think of it as the first light of an oncoming freight train. Behind that initial light are a whole string of weighty concerns, pushing, pushing, pushing. We may ask a very simple question, but there is a great deal hanging in the balance for a response.

Not unlike the rich aristocrat, the disciples want to know about the promise of eternity. They are a bit confounded. All their theories about the everlasting reign of God, one ruled by the messiah, had been shaken by the scene at the temple. Over the past three years, they had learned not to be so crass as to ask if they could possess eternal life. They even grudgingly accepted that they could not lay claim to their seats at the messianic table; at least, not the honoured places. Nevertheless, they did want to understand the general design, to have some inkling concerning the inauguration of Christ's rule.

"What do we look for, Jesus? When will we know that your reign has arrived?" Jesus responds with many surprising tales, all focusing on the contrast between two perspectives of the religious quest for the eternal. There are wise and foolish virgins at a wedding feast. Jesus tells a parable about vigilant and wicked servants who are charged with the running of the household. In this dialogue, we also find the well-known parable of the talents, which juxtaposes blue-chip conservative stewardship with high-rolling, risky stewardship. These contrasting images spell out a common message. Smugness and self-satisfaction are sure ways to miss God's reign. Constant vigilance is required if we are to avoid the trap of self-righteous complacency.

This theme is underlined in the conclusion of his answer to the timing of the reign of God. Jesus tells a parable that is one of his most magnificent and provocative. When the realm of God is inaugurated, there will be a great division of peoples. Like a customs official at an airport, God stands before the press of the crowd, directing some to the left and some to the right. Once divided, God consigns those on the left to eternal damnation. Those on the right go to eternal salvation. Amazingly, no one is able to discern the basis for this division. That's the strikingly disconcerting thread running through the parable. Whether damned or saved, the people don't understand the reasons for their fate.

Even though it's only a story, I can hear the mumbling of the two groups. Looking around at their fellows, feeling poorly used, some heated debates ensue until finally they ask God, "So what's the point. How are we chosen? What makes us alike and what makes our group distinct from the people on your other side?"

God replies, "The saved are those people who ministered to me. Remember when I was hungry? Well, you fed me. How about that thirsty beggar asking for a drink? You bought me a coffee, didn't you? Then there was the ragged bag lady looking for a coat and you took yours off and gave it to me. 'To keep off the chill,' you said. How about those belly-bloated and starving children holding up an empty bowl in expectation? I remember you gave me some bread that day. Or the time you visited me in jail. I was just waiting for a human touch, and you gave it to me."

The good people reply, "When did we ever meet you, God? You weren't there, not really. It was just a bag lady, and the prisoner was a nobody. The children were pictures on television. When did we ever meet you and do all these good things for you?"

The Great Judge responds to these incredulous folk, "In as much as you did it unto the least, you did it unto me!"

121

The damned people are just as mystified as the saved ones. "So when did we not worship you or sing your praises? We're good people, decent folk. We never saw you hungry or thirsty or naked or lonely. If we had seen you in that state, God, we certainly would have come to your aid. Why punish us for what we didn't know?"

God is not moved. "In as much as you did not minister unto the least among you, you did not minister unto me."

What is the point of this parable? Looking beyond the obvious censure of uncharitable people who think they have done the right thing, and the innocence of the unpretentious who, in fact, did do it, I detect a more subtle message. Besides the delineation of what makes for right belief and action, the parable contains a revelation of who God is.

Here is a description of the community of God's reign; a band of people drawn together by the grace implicit within all human suffering. A company of believers who have encountered God in the hungry, the thirsty, the naked, the prisoner, the sick. Think about that. This is an "Ah, ha!" moment—a turning point.

As I noted above, people won't let go of their own accord, or if they do, it is usually the guilt-induced, begrudging kind of giving, which produces paternalistic acts of charity. Relinquishment doesn't begin by reaching for the cheque book; it starts with an encounter with a suffering God, a crucified God.

The first act of stewardship lifestyles' training is the confrontation with God in the pain of this world, among the marginalized and oppressed peoples. Step one, we are met by God and sense a loving graciousness from beyond God's pain. Step two, we find the strength to let go naturally and joyously in order to be present with God. In theological terms, we say that grace precedes faith and righteous works. We love in joyous and spontaneous response to being loved.

In Matthew's last judgement story, Jesus joins the denial of self, or relinquishment, with what I call solidarity with the crucified.

Take a break now. Put this book down and think about the concept of being in solidarity with the people who are crucified in the here and now—around the corner.

Experiential Learning

1. Go have dinner at a soup kitchen. Who is eating there? What is their story?

2. Stop a panhandler on the street. Sit down and find out who they are and why they beg.

3. Join a prison visitation programme and ask yourself who is in prison and why.

Questions for Discussion

1. Who is crucified in your church community, in your family, in your world? Why are they crucified?

2. Read what Mary says about her chosen status in Luke 1:46-56. What is her attitude towards the poor? Is it in sympathy with the parable from Matthew 25?

3. What would it mean for you to stand in solidarity with a crucified person?

4. How do we avoid seeing the beggar and the naked and the thirsty and the hungry person? What mechanisms and ideas has our society constructed to protect us from these people?

Chapter Nine

Beyond Charity: Christ-Centred Solidarity

God has shown the strength of God's arm, scattering the proud in the imagination of their hearts. God has taken the mighty from their thrones and raised up the lowly. God has filled the hungry with good things and has sent the rich away empty handed.

—Mary, the mother of Jesus (Luke 151-53)

The grace by which we are being grasped pushes us toward the world and enables us to begin to act like servants instead of masters. But let us make no mistake about it; this grace does not permit us to regard such stewardship as an option, or merely as one consequence of belief. It is at the centre.

—Hall 1982, 26

Introduction

The charitable reflex arises from the desire to help another in need. We see a poster of hungry children or watch a video clip of starving people and we naturally want to do something. Their desperate circumstances call forth a compassionate response from us. Charity is certainly a virtue, and when I coordinated the activities of an inner-city church mission house, we depended upon the generosity of many people who were moved by nothing other than the virtue of giving so that others might receive.

As it is a virtue, so charity can also become a vice. It can be a way to ignore the real facts and root causes of human misery. Sometimes we write out a cheque in order to relieve ourselves of the real responsibility of resolving crises. Charity can be a mechanism of suppression; a way to make the disturbing pictures of hunger and oppression go away.

All too often, the gifts I received for "the poor people" appeared to be more the result of knee-jerk avoidance than of true charitable compassion. I remember well the morning phone call I received in response to a report of ill-clad children in the city core. A kind man called me, desperate to send down one thousand running shoes. I was overjoyed until he told me they were all for the left foot. He was not a cruel or selfish person. Sometimes the guilt we feel pushes us to immediate and often inappropriate responses. And charity can devolve into oppression: the self-righteous imposition of our social principles on people who have no other choice but to suffer in silence.

There have been times when, under the guise of Christian charity, affluent people have perpetuated the degradation of the poor by handing out food or clothing to the "deserving," while screening out those who didn't meet their moral standards (i.e., drunks, prostitutes, homosexual persons). Unfortunately, this onerous charity can been seen in the way certain food banks operate. As government social programmes are "rationalized," middle-class people jump into the breech to supply food to the hungry. All too often the result is another unofficial welfare system that checks out people's "suitability" for charity before food is given—an unnecessarily degrading practice.

It is because of these and other distortions of well-intentioned benevolence that I promise myself I will never commit charity again! Without some deeper motivation than either guilt or desperation, Christian charity is a frightening thing to behold and even more deadly to receive.

Given these disturbing dimensions of charity, I link relinquishment with solidarity; letting go in order to stand with the marginalized. In fact, I will suggest that solidarity leads naturally to relinquishment, standing with the outsiders in order to let go. I call this solidarity Christ-centred.

"Solidarity" has become a plastic word. It is often used as a quick response to cover any number of actions. As it has a progressive tone, it often gets tacked onto prayers and petitions without due regard for its essential meaning. This chapter will define it within a theological context and enable us to avoid any stretched or vague use of the concept.

Christ-Centred Solidarity: Meeting the Broken God

I have mentioned that one reason we are prepared to accept the ethic of acquisition as the *modus operandi* of our North American existence is that we have fashioned a God who suits that lifestyle. In the first place, our accountant deity demands that we work hard, control our desires, and strive to achieve spiritual perfection. In this existence, there is no joy in giving away—no joy in living, for that matter. Under the weight of the Protestant work ethic, life is limited to a sober climb to inner purity and outward restraint. That's all there is: self-control and social sobriety.

In the second place, this all-powerful, all-knowing, detached "Sky God" lets the children hoard and fight over their toys in the earthly sandbox because what is really important is not found down here anyway. This is just kindergarten. The real school happens after death in the reign of heaven. So you can get all you want right now because you won't have to account for your reckoning until you get to God's throne room on high. Even then it's not such a serious offense to have hoarded the earth's fruits, since righteousness is a matter of one's soul and its purity (read "sexual" purity).

In the final place, our God is a tight-fisted, demanding deity, who rewards sexual virtue and punishes insolence or foolishness. There is no room for play, no place in this God's heart for extravagant grace. There is reward for good deeds and punish-

126

ment for misdemeanours. That's all. With this God, there is no inspiration to let go. Perish the thought! Charity is part and parcel of the hard-nosed business of rewards. We give only what we need to give to get our heavenly crown. End of argument. End of stewardship.

While all descriptions of God are only metaphors and not important in the final analysis, the way we speak of the transcendent does influence how we live our lives. If God is detached from creation, believers will tend to have little regard for the earth and its preservation. If God is "tight," we become tight. If God is a "let's make a deal" deity who exchanges blessings for good behaviour, we shape our lives accordingly. We fashion our lives according to the goal we seek, in the goal captured by the metaphors we use to describe God.

Now, here's my question: What would it mean to accept as our primary theological metaphor that God is best revealed in hungry people? Ask yourself: Would our Sunday worship change if we prayed with all our hearts and minds to a God who is thirsty and naked and alone? How about our prayer meetings? Could believers gather together to commune with a God who is imprisoned and sick?

It sounds strange, even scandalous, as a suggestion, but is this not the very core of our faith tradition? Is this not the lesson of the second stewardship workshop, that God is found in the strangest and most destitute people? The parable of the last judgement found in Matthew 25 departs from the traditional image of God at this very crucial point, even though it has many striking similarities with the common assumptions concerning divine power and judgement. Rather than speaking of God as all powerful, it reveals a God who comes begging. It sounds preposterous, but the parable points to a deity embodied in sickness, starvation, thirst, and imprisonment. What a strange image of God! Can this be our God, the one we claim is "almighty" and "victorious"?

Let us assume that God is not capricious, that God did not cast lots when determining how to appear to human beings. Let us assume that God's choice was and is intentional. God chooses to be known in a specific way because it is in this fashion that humankind can truly understand the divine. If this is the case, then the parable of the last judgement is a logical extension of God as revealed in the crucified Jesus of Nazareth. If Christ is at the centre of our faith, then in Christ's cross we confront a God who seeks to be known as a broken being—suffering, humiliated, destitute, and abandoned—the message of the parable from Matthew.

In his novel *Silence*, Shusaku Endo gives modern expression to this image of a broken God. In a poignant passage, the Japanese author describes the plight of a Portuguese priest, Sebastian, who has travelled to Japan to be a missionary. He is following his master and teacher to that country and arrives just in time for the great persecution of Christians that took place in Japan in the seventeenth century.

Sebastian has always been plagued with a devotional handicap. He prays constantly to Jesus and is able to visualize his Saviour in the greatest detail, but his Jesus never speaks, never offers the slightest word of comfort. Christ is always silent, hence the title of the novel. Sebastian suffers many hardships during the persecution, but adamantly resists the pressure to apostatize, even though his Christ gives no direction and offers no solace.

After many hardships, Sebastian is no longer able to hold out. In Endo's story, Sebastian's apostasy required that he trample on an image of Christ. The authorities placed an image of Christ's face attached to a wooden board before the priest. Sebastian contemplates this face upon which he is about to step and thereby renounce his trust and faith in God. Looking upon the bruised and trampled Jesus, he speaks to his Saviour. His prayer is a petition for a blessing, for some message of hope. Silence! Christ does not speak. Heartbroken and discouraged, Sebastian abandons all hope and begins the motions to renounce his faith.

The priest raises his foot. In it he feels a dull, heavy pain. This is no formality. He will now trample on what he believed most pure, on what is filled with the ideals and dreams of man. How his foot aches! And then the Christ in bronze speaks to the priest. "Trample! Trample! I more than anyone know of the pain in your foot. Trample! It was to be trampled on by men that I was born into this world. It was to share men's pain that I carried my cross" (Endo 1976, 259).

Is it possible for Christians to believe in such a God, one who comes into the world precisely to be trampled on? Can we put our faith in a God who so loves the world that participation in its pain is the starting point for divine revelation and action? What would such an image of God do to our notions of piety and obedience? Isn't this a twisted, even masochistic, image of the divine?

These are all excellent questions, but my primary focus is on stewardly discipleship. So I ask you: What does the suffering God mean for our understanding of stewardship and our passion for possessions and the possessing spirit? How does this crucified God help us to let go?

First, this image of the crucified God re-orients our understanding of charity. We are not called upon to give to the poor because they are "deserving" or "less fortunate" than we are. We give to the poor because we recognize that God is somehow especially visible in their midst. Transcendence is revealed in a unique way among the dispossessed, among the ones who are trampled upon. God is in their midst as God is not in the midst of the comfortable and affluent. In this sense, relinquishment opens a spiritual window of opportunity.

According to the revelation of Jesus Christ on the cross, if we would see God, touch eternity, or participate in God's salvation, then we must somehow enter into the world of those who suffer. The faith journey begins among the diminished of this world, in their suffering. There is no other route. A Jewish proverb explains this well: "Some people cannot see God because they won't bend down low enough."

If we believe in this low God, then our charity to the lowly is really a prayer of supplication. If God is truly to be found among the dispossessed, then it is a deeply spiritual act to move beyond charitable acts aimed at the poor and find some space in which we may live with them and accept the burden of solidarity: to make their suffering our suffering, their injustice our injustice, their starvation, powerlessness, and oppression our own. Of course, solidarity with the poor has political and economic connotations. Nevertheless, Christ-centred solidarity is initially a spiritual undertaking.

In his description of "the theology of the cross," Martin Luther maintained that there is no other starting point for the pilgrimage to meet God than on the road of God's suffering in the world. Admittedly, this may sound a trifle bizarre or masochistic—another male response to the quest for God. Luther did not expect Christians to inflict suffering on themselves or to rush out in search of pain. Rather, if we stand with those who are in pain and look at the world through their experience, then we will come to understand the depth of God's loving presence. Solidarity, standing with, is the key. It does not allow for self-serving asceticism. It does not tolerate egotistical martyrdom.

Charity can lead us to this solidarity. The gift given in love draws us into the lives who receive it, and hence to a greater appreciation of their plight and, finally, to that point where their suffering becomes our own. But this is all still theory. I want to get to the encounter. Solidarity with God's pain never walks up to you on the street. God usually takes the form of a person, a hurting man, a destitute woman.

Let me explain how I was converted. I met Diane, the mother of three children. She lived down the street from me in an old, rundown tenement building. It was eight-thirty in the morning when she came to my door. I had heard that there had been a fire in her flat, but that's all I knew. Diane came to the office breathless, with tears streaming down her face. Not only had she lost everything in the fire, but her youngest child, an eighteen-month-old boy, was also dead. The fire had reached the back of her apartment before she could get the lad out.

Diane was on welfare and she came to me because folks had told her that I knew the rights of those on social assistance. She had no money, but she heard that welfare would do something to help out in times of crisis. Could I help?

We went immediately to the local office. It just so happened that, in this office, the worker in charge of emergencies was also responsible for detecting fraudulent cases. Often he would mix the two functions, seeking to gain information on cheaters while he dealt with people who were desperate—a potentially fortuitous and cruel combination. It was his job to visit the scenes of all fires in our area to determine if assistance was needed, so I knew he was already well acquainted with Diane's troubles.

While we sat waiting for this bureaucrat to appear, Diane talked of her lost son, of all the broken dreams. She couldn't believe he was gone. She wept.

Her worker entered with no word of greeting, no comforting remarks. He didn't even apologize for having to pose awkward questions. He began by asking who the male was who had been in the apartment overnight. He also asked her why she been able to save her other two children and not this third one. He was accusing her of sleeping around and neglecting her children. Diane was speechless and trembling and the questions kept coming. "Isn't it strange that the fire started in the front and went all the way to the back but didn't go upstairs? Why is that? Who was that fellow that left just as I was arriving on the scene?"

I can still feel anger well up inside me when I recall that interview. In Diane, I saw the pain of God written large, in her utter helplessness before an unfeeling man and an evil system. Guilt and shame and grief were all wrapped into one as she suffered under the glare of that accusing bureaucrat. It was because of that encounter with Diane that I began to recognize God's yearning for a new world, for a just system. I could see dimly the God who chose to come to this planet to be with the downtrodden. That was God's preferred position; that is where God is to be found, on the beggars' side of the counter.

Of course, solidarity with that broken God who stands with

the powerless in their abandonment, who suffers humiliation along with those who are shamed, implies that the disciples will likewise be broken. In this sense, baptism into the community of Christ could be understood as initiation into the company of the crucified ones. Is that a frightening prospect? It is for me. No one wants to be crucified.

Christians have become so accustomed to hanging crosses everywhere, on church buildings, around our necks, that we don't see the absolute scandal of that symbol, its shame and humiliation. This cross is not some ornament to be worn as jewellery. It is not a secret charm to be lifted up like some triumphant sign of victory. It is an instrument of torture, a rack that breaks and starves its victims; not a pretty sight, not a pretty company, this company of the cross. This cross is an unnerving revelation of a God who loves.

When we erect a cross on our church buildings, we are telling the wider community that we're open and available to all those who are tortured and punished. Here's a place for the outsiders. The cross is a billboard pointing to a sanctuary for the marginalized and lost. We're declaring that we stand with everyone who is shamefully treated, with all those who have no safe place, no bread or clothes. A cross is like a great neon sign blinking out, "We stand with the lowest of the low. This house is your house."

If Christian stewardship lifestyles begin with an encounter that moves us into solidarity with those who are crucified, imagine how our communities would change! If we took that encounter and that solidarity seriously, how much would we be transformed?

Solidarity: The Emergence of a New Community

Christians are challenged, through their faith in a broken God who erects a cross in the midst of the dispossessed, to make the poor and the dispossessed the motivation of their relinquishment. The marginalized, and God living through them, become the *raison d'etre* of stewardly discipleship.

Such an orientation turns relinquishment from an essentially self-serving guilt reflex into an inspired and sincere act of self-sacrifice. Now relinquishment has a purpose, that of being a natural, even joyful, response to the God who suffers. Gandhi once said, "A mother would never, by choice, sleep in a wet bed, but she would gladly do so in order to spare the dry bed for her child." Has not Gandhi captured the inner wisdom of relinquishment? When letting go is linked with and instigated by solidarity, when we choose to respond to the suffering of another, our letting go is an authentic and freeing response. Through participation in the liberation of those who are dispossessed, we, the possessors, are liberated from our own consuming spirit.

Gandhi's wisdom aside, the notion of solidarity as I have explained it appears to be one of the central precepts of the prophetic side of the biblical record. The Hebrew prophets, including John the Baptist and Jesus, are not concerned with the intrinsic virtue of wealthy or poor people. Rather, what seems to capture their full imagination is what wealthy people do or don't do for the poor. That is the measure by which a community of the faithful is judged; indeed, how any economic or political structure is evaluated. We are to look to the poor, to the outsiders, the people with no rights, and ask how they are treated, why they are oppressed. Therein lies the test of our righteousness.

According to the testimony of Jesus, it is for this reason that the community of the faithful are marked by their actions in relation to the outcasts and not according to their piety or moral righteousness. According to Jesus, disciples are those folk who venture out among the lost, forgotten, and marginalized and take up their lot, making the struggles of the forgotten their own struggles. For it is in their striving for justice that God is most authentically present.

This solidarity with the disenfranchised, as sign of the faithful community, will quite necessarily convert the church to a new way of being. Through such an association with those on the margins of our society, the church itself will be marginalized. Making common cause with the rejects of society, it will no longer be considered a trustworthy proponent of the status quo. The church will lose its respectable role as spiritual mascot for the affluent.

For many believers, a serious shift towards solidarity will make the church unappealing, even frightening. For it has been a safe and secure dwelling place where traditional (self-congratulatory and comfortable) values are proclaimed. This will be the case no longer. Solidarity will turn the church into a company of the cross, a gathering of people committed to the establishment of "kingdom" values and standards that uphold justice over propriety, and love over efficiency.

If the church holds to these values, it will soon lose those marks of status that it has often enjoyed: economic security, political privilege, and social respectability. The company of the cross would not be asked to pray at the President's conference or the Prime Minister's breakfast. There will be no special dispensation given by City Hall. We'll have to start paying municipal taxes.

Similarly, the act of solidarity quite naturally forces a choice. I wish it were not so, but in an imperfect world, we cannot avoid reality. Solidarity with the poor will push the church into their company and out of the world of the wealthy. More often than we might like, the cross-bearing community of faith will be lumped in with the rejects, the lunatics and untouchables. At that juncture, the church will have to make a choice. Where does its loyalty lie: with "all" people, which in reality means with those who pay the bills, or with the disenfranchised of society, who by their very nature cannot afford anything? This is not an easy decision. The powerful will not want the church to make its bed with the poor, preferring that it minister to all classes of society. Unfortunately, in the short term at least, this is not possible. To be on the side of the dispossessed means that one is against those who possess too much.

This will be a difficult time for an institution that has understood itself to be a champion of impartiality. Even though this neutrality has often been biased in favour of the powerful, the necessity of taking a clear option for the side of the poor, as opposed to that of the non-poor, will be traumatic. Our partiality will by its very nature force, or result in, a reduction in size and a dwindling of ecclesiastical resources. In a phrase, if the church adopts this model of stewardly discipleship as solidarity, it will become disestablished. No longer the church of empire, it will become the company of the catacombs, existing in the shadows for the people who are frightened, hiding and lost.

It is in the awareness of the consequences of stewardship solidarity that we now recognize that the faith of the cross is not about "all things bright and beautiful," at least not for the powerful, white, male establishment. Worshipping the crucified saviour will mean following Jesus as he is crucified in the thousands of homeless people living in boxes and sleeping on subway grates. Can we stand by him as he is scourged in the single black mother who prostitutes herself to earn money for her children? Are we able to walk with Jesus as he is humiliated in the northern Innu chief who sold his birthright for a dubious dosage of Northern technology?

In light of the need for genuine solidarity, the stewardship lifestyle I describe will be difficult and demanding, with little tranquillity. We will be asked to stand where we feel uncomfortable and walk in embarrassing places. We may go to jail with those who protest their cause in civil disobedience.

Now I have to admit that the prospect of solidarity frightens me. It threatens my livelihood, property, and position. If I am asked to give anything up, it's my status as a powerful, white male that I would find most difficult to relinquish, for then I would be nothing. I wish with all my heart that this was not the call of the gospel.

There are many times when I hide in spiritual rationalizations or political ignorance. I run to my hectic schedule and escape through business. Many join me in this effort to flee from the ever-convincing, yet highly demanding, challenge of the gospel. It's like a conspiracy: as long as we all run hard and blind, we'll never have to face the world as it is. We feel very much like the disciples looking at the needle and the camel: "Solidarity—it's impossible."

Solidarity: The Grasp of Grace

The impossibility of relinquishment leads us naturally to another aspect of stewardship lifestyles that evolves into solidarity. The act of giving away, of letting go for the sake of the dispossessed, is essentially impossible in any real sense without the action of God. That may sound pious and empty, but I mean two things by it.

First, we are a forgiven people. Believe it! As Paul Tillich, a man who knew whereof he spoke, said once, "Accept that you are accepted even though you feel unacceptable!"

Of course, affluent North Americans are the earth's problem, as we are the ones who consume more than anyone else, greedily demanding much more than our fair share. Nevertheless, we are called out of this vicious and frustrating life. We are set free for another purpose. Since we have a tight grasp on the rope of life and will not let go easily, God must let go for us. It is the grace-filled forgiveness of the suffering God that allows us to trust, to let go, to give up in favour of solidarity.

In this regard, I am reminded of the prayer of a sixty-year-old citizen of Washington, who helps out in the food kitchen run by the Sojourner's community. Mrs. Mary Glover prays as someone who knows to whom she is talking as she says, "Lord, we know that you'll be coming through this line today, so help us to treat you well." We are given the grace to relinquish because God calls out of misery, pleading for all we can give.

Hence, in relinquishment inspired by Christ-centred solidarity, we witness a mysterious transaction of power. The powerful release their grip because they have seen the truth of life as manifested in the powerless; the beauty of a life lived not for having, but for being. We can see and feel it. There is a deep centredness in the existence of those who address the struggles of life from the position of vulnerability, such as Jean Vanier, Mother Theresa, Mahatma Gandhi, Dorothy Day, Oscar Romero.

Secondly, the grace of God, embodied in the dispossessed, grasps believers. It does not cuddle! It elicits an ethical response propelling humanity through the eye of the needle. This grace will not let us slide out from under the challenge of the cross of solidarity as if it were a special elective reserved only for the truly serious believer. The grace of God pushes us towards the world to be "servants instead of masters."

Christ-centred solidarity, then, is not a result of our personal determination or the church's courageous actions. While solidarity depends upon these things, it is primarily a consequence of God's grace. Without the primary dependence upon grace, our relinquishment would be a bitter act and our solidarity would taste of self-righteousness.

Take note, those of you who would be Christ's followers and who desire to be freed from the possessing spirit: our chief pitfalls in the work of building up stewardly lifestyles are self-righteousness and bitterness. They eat away at the eager mind and turn hearts to stone.

While relinquishment coupled with solidarity is a daunting task for stewardly discipleship, there is yet one more aspect of "letting go" to be explored. Just as the disciples moved from the cross to the empty tomb, so stewardly discipleship must move beyond suffering and encompass some appreciation of hope. Expectancy, a stewardship vision for ourselves and our community, becomes the central theme of the third and final stewardship workshop led by Jesus of Nazareth, explored in the next chapter.

Experiential Learning

1. Do an analysis of your town, city, or suburb. Ask yourself who the powerful people are and why they are that way. Ask who the powerless ones are and why they live as they do. Now ask yourself: Who stands with the powerless? Is your church or religious community standing with them in some way? What are the avenues towards solidarity with them?

What are their goals and hopes? What would it mean for your community of faith to take on the same hopes and goals?

2. Place yourself in the company of the crucified. Discover for yourself who they are. They live in every region of North America. Who are they and how can you stand with them?

Questions for Discussion

1. Who is our neighbour? How can their struggle become our own?

2. What does the Bible say about solidarity? Think of the people with whom Jesus worked and ask what he did with them that angered the religious authorities.

3. Who are marginalized within your church? For what reason?

Chapter Ten

The Passion for Expectancy: Stewardship as Living Hope

Those who hope for hope ... are entitled to do so only if they have measured that which has the power to obscure hope, only if they have lived in the shadow of utter denial.

—Wiesel 1969, vi

Introduction

Sunday evening bingo can be so frustrating! It was held every week in the church around the corner from the community centre where I was once involved in community organizing.

Thinking back, I recall how I would spend many hours on the phone, walking the streets, knocking on door after door, meeting new people, encouraging first-time members, and reassuring loyal supporters, to ensure that a reasonable crowd appeared for the current project, demonstration, negotiation session, or planning meeting.

On a good week, one hundred people might join in a picket line and fifty might appear for a press conference. While these figures may not be impressive by U.S. standards, in "law and order" Canada, one hundred people on the street was something akin to chaos. Nevertheless, it was hard work—not like getting people out for bingo!

Every Sunday night, without invitation, without telephone reminders, without even a flier announcing it, eight hundred to one thousand people made their way to the church hall for bingo. It still happens in the high-tech 1990s. How often I fantasize about that crowd. What if the bingo game were turned into a protest rally on sub-standard housing or low welfare rates or child poverty? If one hundred people could make things move, imagine what a thousand could do.

As far as I know, bingo never evolves into revolution, but a question lingers: Why do the poor and disenfranchised show up for bingo games they rarely win but not for public meetings that often prove informative, if not profitable?

I find some solace in the realization that, without a doubt, demonstrations are more risky than bingo. After all, no one has been arrested or forced from their apartment for playing bingo. There are more practical reasons for its popularity. For many women, the game is an excuse for a social night away from the oppressive situation at home: lack of resources, crowded living quarters, abusive males, daily boredom. Here they can control a small piece of their lives, complain openly about their lot in life, compare horror stories about their partners, have a good time among friends. It's also a diversion. In the frenzy of the moment, when the cards fill up anxiously close to the big win, they forget their troubles.

Although it does sound a bit farfetched, some avid players maintain that playing bingo is also fulfilling a religious duty. The money goes to the church, and so they are just helping out a needy cause; being good stewards by spending their entertainment money in the service of God.

In spite of all these practical reasons, I believe the real attraction of bingo is that it offers an evening of hope. The big cash prizes are merely symbols of this hope. People stream to the bingo hall because they hope to win that final big prize. Everyone has a dream of what they will do with that windfall. Great expectations fill the hall, as thick as the cigarette smoke. Each player breathes in hope; to make a new start, to turn things around. Whenever you ask people why they go, the possibility of winning is their first response. This much said, there is more to the hope offered by bingo than the prizes.

It is a game of expectancy. Its addictive quality is clear. Each player comes very close to winning in almost every game. So you're sure, absolutely sure, that the next game will be your lucky one. Hope dances across the cards of each player as the numbers are called out. It is the energy of expectancy that makes bingo popular. The game is doubly attractive to the marginalized community because the bingo hall is a different, hope-inspired environment. Here is a wish-world where someone is always winning. If only on one night of the week, if for only one fleeting moment, people live in hope.

Those hundreds in the bingo hall embody the truth that, besides food and shelter, human beings require some measure of hope in order to survive. Bingo mania is matched by casinos and video gambling. As faith in the effectiveness of social projects declines (as is now the case), games of chance increase in popularity. The slogan is true: If there is no vision, the people perish. So if there is no hope to be found in religious practice, people will manufacture it elsewhere.

Surely those who would live a stewardly life are no different than bingo players. We also need hope. The reluctance to relinquish described in previous chapters is fed by our inability to hope. Solidarity will be impossible, that conversion will not happen, if, in the process, disciples of Christ cannot hope past their doubts and fears to some greater vision.

I have chosen to speak of hope or expectancy (for the sake of this chapter these words are used interchangeably) after the topics of relinquishment and solidarity because this is its proper theological place. Easter comes after Good Friday, resurrection follows crucifixion, and hope emerges only through the confrontation with the pain of solidarity and the struggle to let go.

If the progression of ideas is reversed or short-circuited, as is often the case in an "optimistic" society and in our over-eager church, we do not find real hope. Rather, it is a cheap version that seeks to reflect only one aspect of expectancy—that of wishful thinking or "superficial beliefullness" (Hall 1986, 27). In contrast to this preliminary, superficial hoping, the gospel calls us to real hope, deep and mature. It is not primarily an emotion that is felt so much as it is a reality that is lived.

Let's turn now to the third workshop in Christian stewardship and explore this point.

Workshop Three: The Mystery of Expectancy

This workshop begins on a dusty and dreary road, where two companions travel on their way out of Jerusalem. Known as the story of the road to Emmaus, and recounted only in the Gospel of Luke (Luke 24: 13-35; Mark 16:13 contains a passing reference to two travellers), we know little about the actual facts surrounding this most striking post-resurrection appearance by Jesus. We can't pin-point a geographic location for Emmaus. Experts cite four possible locations, each with its own historical and theological twist. We know one traveller was Cleopas, but who was the other? Were they both apostles, family members (tradition suggests that Cleopas was the uncle of Jesus), or friends?

I have always been puzzled by their reason for leaving the Holy City at this precise moment. Why were these two out walking on this first Easter? Were they discouraged by the crucifixion? Had they given up on the hopeless and hapless band of Jesus' followers who lingered around the upper room? Was the way to Emmaus a road of despair or disillusionment?

The walkers might have been working off nervous energy, stretching their legs because they couldn't stand the waiting. How could they sit still? Hearing the rumours of a resurrection, listening to the women speak in a tumble of song and dance, how could they tolerate the tension of wondering? They wanted to believe that the Lord was alive and yet they didn't want to face the twelve if these glimmers of hope proved false.

Then again, this journey might have been decided upon in haste. Perhaps they were running, fleeing the threat of Roman persecution. The mood among the authorities was ugly and Pilate had crushed many messiah movements in the past. There was no time to lose. Emmaus was the route of escape.

Whatever the reason, these two were on their way, talking vigorously. While they are deep in debate, a stranger joins them. How true it is that the great teachers and the great insights of our lives walk up to us from behind. Looking in another direction, the shining revelations that mean so much appear to be beside the point; they meet us looking like foreigners.

Through discussion, this unknown figure begins to reveal the wisdom of the prophecy concerning God's presence on earth and God's purpose for creation. The road to Emmaus becomes a sparkling seminar. Luke records: "Did not our hearts burn within us as he talked on the road?" Whoever he was, he inspired the two companions with an exciting, soul-inflaming vision.

Even though he was obviously a very provocative and engaging speaker, the two travellers did not know him as Jesus. It is only after they persuade him to join them for dinner that, in the breaking of bread, he is revealed to them as the Christ.

My second question for Luke is: How could they have been so blind? Were they so dense that they couldn't even recognize their master and former teacher? They had been with the master for three years, and here, they do not know him. "What fools," we say. "Surely we would have recognized him!" However, we must guard against our derision. Jesus walks with us often, and we don't see him, do we?

The climax of the story is that the two finally discover who Jesus is. This is the Lord, the one we long to see. Here is our master, who gives us a sustaining hope through the simple act of breaking bread.

Whatever Luke may want to say about the nature of knowing and spiritual enlightenment, in this account we see enacted a marvellous lesson concerning the fundamental structures of the community of faith. Faith begins as a journey of deep debate, and the church is a body that is overtaken in its good intentions by a mystery that sets hearts on fire with vision. The community of

Christ's disciples is established by spirit-filled visions—in the breaking of daily bread and the acknowledgement of our Saviour. It is a body of hopeless and blind travellers who constantly search for the divine presence in their midst.

Finally, the Emmaus road is a fitting metaphor for the church and assuredly for the disciple who would live a stewardly lifestyle, for it leads from Calvary's hill into a mysterious, unknown land. Discipleship is always "on the way," and never a completed task, and we cannot presume to have understood it all or achieved a finished state. The story of Emmaus teaches the gathered that we live by daily bread and each day we seek again for its sustenance and test its vision.

Without hope and vision, any attempt to follow the path of the cross as I have described it, from solidarity to relinquishment, would be like the seed that falls among the stones, springing up quickly only to wither and die for lack of sustaining nourishment. The life lived in solidarity with the dispossessed, a life in which relinquishment becomes a natural and joyous "letting go," can't be sustained if there is not an intertwining thread of expectancy. I know I won't relinquish anything and I won't stand by anyone if I don't have hope. Hope is the jewel of great price, the treasure hid in the field (Matt. 13:44, 46).

Whatever it may have lost or corrupted over two millennia, the miracle of the Christian Church is that it still keeps expectancy alive. When the collective will to create a new world is tattered and torn in a swirling sea of cynicism, the community of faith is at least a haven for those who want to find real hope. Living by the gospel story, believers expect God to appear in their world, no matter how destitute their situation. They hope for a new world to come, even when the present one seems lost.

I believe the Emmaus story reveals that expectancy takes two forms: hope and vision. While they are intertwined, they also deserve to be outlined and understood separately. There is the hope that is intrinsic to human becoming or what I loosely call ontological hope, which I will explore further here. And there is a hope that is more like a directing vision or what I refer to as "eschatological" hope: hope concerning the "eschaton," the last things, that great age promised by Christ, which I will take up in the next chapter.

Hope as Becoming

If we examine the example of bingo carefully, we come to see that the hope involved is not simply wishful thinking. If this were so, bingo would soon lose its appeal. Players would ask themselves, "How many games must I lose?" Superficial optimism would quickly wither as the wait for the "big" win extended into months and years. People would cease to play the game. Bingo proves that hope is more than an emotional state or a fanciful fixation. In its essence, hope is an essential part of human living, a triumph of human becoming. It's like food and drink. We need it to survive.

To speak technically for a moment, I believe that all human beings experience their lives through an opposition of several "polar tensions." The most obvious is the tension between being a separate individual and being part of a group. All our lives we live between these two seemingly opposing desires. Recognizing the self as a separate being is indispensable in the maturation from infancy into adulthood. If we do not embrace distinct selfhood, we stay as children, dependent on our parents. So we strive to be unique and separate, because otherwise we die. At the same time, everyone longs to be part of a group. In fact, much of our life's vocation is taken up with the unending search for communion with others. In adolescence we use fads and fashions to be considered "cool" and acceptable to the gang, but it doesn't end with the teen years. Throughout our adult life, we yearn for partnership, communion, relationship, all states of living that bring us into intimacy with another. All humans intuit that there is a unity from which we came and towards which we strain. Under the constraints of time and space, this unity can only be grasped in fragments through human relationships. Nevertheless, we need community desperately.

Can you can see it? Can you feel the tension? It's probably at the top of every teenager's list of anxiety-producing thoughts: "How can I be me and yet be part of a group?" Humans need both separateness and unity and how do we get both? To be human is to be caught in this indissoluble tension. If there is a bridge between the two poles it is found in love: a love that is not afraid to allow for distinctiveness, a love whose self-hood is not damaged by unity with the beloved nor devastated by separation. This love comes as a gift; some would say it comes from God.

The striving between separation and unity is not the only tension we live through as human creatures. There is a second tension, one between history and freedom. In this context, I define history as the collection of all our life's conditions, our environmental influences, our parentage, and our cultural heritage, all that has combined to make us what we are. At the other end of the scale is the unique human capacity to break from the dictates of history into freedom and the capacity to see the potentialities within daily living. Call it "what if" vision: what if peace were possible, what if we loved one another, what if we outlawed poverty or violence.

Like separateness and unity, history and freedom are in tension with each other. Everyone needs history, an awareness of rootedness. If we lacked history, we would have to rise each morning and form our self-identity anew. That would be an impossible burden. In contrast, everyone has, and needs to exercise, their freedom. Can you imagine what life would be like without surprises, without the possibility of deciding to do a new thing? A world without freedom would be the making of our worst nightmares—Orwell's 1984 revisited!

History and freedom are joined. We need them both. If we ignore history and accentuate freedom (and that seems to be the trend in our society), we consign ourselves to a hectic, baseless existence in which there is a constant striving to re-make ourselves in a new way. That sounds very much like the bronze life I described earlier. By concentrating on freedom, human beings discover that each moment becomes the moment when they must decide afresh what it is to be who we are. While it may be initially quite liberating, such a rootless existence is finally soul destroying, since each new moment cannot bear the full weight of life's meaning and purpose. Consequently human beings require more than freedom. We need roots in order to survive as there must be a base from which to work and decide. If we live only for freedom, we do not become. Rather, we overdose on fantasy.

Conversely, a life that ignores freedom and is based solely on history is equally deadening. Without the possibility of a break from the past, we suffocate, as the fresh air of new beginnings is cut off. Life becomes an enormous rut, a banal existence that kills the child-like playfulness and innocence we harbour within us.

If we are to grow into the fullness of our humanity, then we must appreciate and exercise a choice over both history and freedom and keep them in some balance. This is not easy, since these two poles are pulling us in opposite directions. How do we find the necessary equilibrium? A balance between freedom and history is not sustained through dint of intellectual or emotional effort. Rather, there is a mysterious gift that dwells within us, so mysterious that, as a Christian, I sense its source is the divine. This is the gift of hope.

Hope is not a logical concept. It makes no real sense, since it does not come into our hearts simply because we feel expectant or optimistic. It also arises in spite of our hopelessness. Often at the very point when we are most painfully in touch with our helplessness, hope appears and grows within us like a miraculous antidote to despair. I sense it is this gift of hope that allows us to retain a wholesome balance between our appreciation of rootedness and a constant longing for what is new.

Given its essential place in human existence, I believe hope is a step on the road to becoming. Mastering the inner tension between history and freedom is part of growing into maturity. Hope, then, is an important motive power that helps us to live with this tension and pushes us into new life.

It should not surprise believers that the biblical record portrays healthy and wholesome human life as hopeful living. (See Job 19:21-27; Ps. 77, 90, 102, 121.) Living hope is best portrayed in the Judeo-Christian tradition in the image of manna from heaven. We all know the famous tale. Each day the children of Yahweh, wandering in the wilderness, received bread from the skies. They could not hoard it nor store it up. They lived each day both with their historic need for bread and their expectancy that God would send food. In a very concrete way, hope was woven into the fabric of living. It was this daily hope that shaped the nomadic slaves from Egypt into the people of God.

Surely this is the point of Jesus' petition to "give us this day our daily bread." Human existence stands under the sign of manna, which, according to Exodus 16, appears each morning as a gift from God to those who trust the Lord, even though they wander through the wilderness.

What would our world be like if we had to live by this hope? What would it mean for pension funds, annuities, deep freezes, and the multitude of schemes designed to help us store up our bread for a rainy day? Could it be that the ethic guiding stewardly discipleship is the ethic of daily bread-daily hoping? Was this not one of the allusions fixed by Christ in the eucharistic act that opened the eyes of the Emmaus pilgrims?

Daily-bread hope is born in the night, as we await the sunrise of new day. It is the pre-dawn attire of a Christian disciple. We who follow Christ must live and grow with this moment-by-moment expectancy; the capacity, nay, the passion, to live on intimate terms with neediness and to receive sustenance each day from God. It is the courage to hope for "enough," not more nor less that we need, just enough! Without this daily hope, relinquishment is impossible, and solidarity is a facade. Without this manna-in-the-wilderness hope, we will become overwhelmed by the call to solidarity, fall into despair, and burn out.

We are free to share all that we have with our neighbours, and free to suffer in solidarity with our brothers and sisters when they cry out, precisely because we live by the gift of daily hope, acknowledging our need and expecting God's care. Then and only then does relinquishment become a joy and solidarity a wondrous opportunity to see the face of God.

The first aspostles of Jesus lived by this daily hope, accepting that life was not something to be grasped or held, that it could only be lived through the hope that trusts in manna. John Chrysostom, one of the great preachers of that early church, proclaimed the life lived by hope when he said: "We received all things from Christ. Existence itself we have through Him, and life and breath and light and air and earth....We are sojourners and pilgrims. All this about mine and thine is mere verbiage and does not stand for reality since the very air, earth, matter are the Creator's and so are you too" (Avila 1983, 1). It remains to be seen if twentieth-century disciples can reappropriate this wisdom of the founding leaders.

There is one final aspect to what I describe as daily-bread hoping. It is not mere fantasy, "whistling in the dark" hopefulness, nor is it the pretence of optimism that is found in our North American culture—the "happy ever after" of fairy tales. The Israelites in the wilderness knew these harsh facts. They lived by the hope of manna, but they were not constantly joyous and free from anxiety or doubt. In fact, they were often angry and afraid, feeling lost and helpless. Each day as they gathered the bread of heaven, they faced the spectre of a tomorrow with no food in sight, no reserves upon which to draw. It wasn't easy or pleasant!

Manna hope, the kind of hope that lasts and builds us into full human creatures, is found on the other side of our hopelessness. It is found when we have nothing left to which to return, upon which to rely, when the night falls and our bread has run out. Costly hope is not found in the light, but appears only after we face the shadows.

Experiential Learning

1. Organize a pilgrimage for your church community. Decide on a route and take only as much as you can carry. Organize it to suit the participants, but explore what daily-bread hoping is like on a foot journey together. You might undertake the pilgrimage as a part of lenten devotion or as a form of

summer activity. As a community, try to live by having all things in common, depending upon the hospitality of those you meet on the way.

Questions for Discussion

1. Read the Exodus account of manna and ask whether we could live that way in our culture.

2. How could the church community become a place where we live with what we have, not asking for more than our share?

3. Individually, define the idea of hope. What does it mean for your life? Now share the different images of hope. How do they differ? Compare your descriptions to what the Bible says about hope.

Chapter Eleven

Our Vision: Some Steps along the Stewardship Pathway

Always be prepared to make a defence to anyone who calls you to account for the hope that is in you.

—1 Peter 3:15

Introduction

Ontological hope is not the only hope there is. The Christian tradition has more to say, much more. The gospel speaks of a lively hope, the kind that lifts us up and inspires us through acts of solidarity and relinquishment. This second kind of hope is more than daily-bread hope. It is a dancing hope, an eager and excited hope that strains towards an object, a vision.

Saint Ambrose, a teacher of Saint Augustine, said that "we lose things which are common when we claim things as our own." In our possessive and possessing world, one common object that has been lost is vision: a way of seeing how the world might be.

If you've been plodding through these pages wondering when we were going to get to the heart of the matter, look no further. In this chapter we will explore the vision of what a stewardly lifestyle might look like for us and for our communities. We've arrived at the most demanding aspect of stewardly discipleship: exploring the vision that inspires our solidarity and our relinquishment.

151

When those two travellers walked the dusty road to Emmaus, they were set on fire by the stranger's insight into the scriptures and by his vision for the time ahead. Let us join them in their journey and discover what awaits us.

The Vision List

It would take volumes to explore all of the possibilities of a Christian vision for our world. At this point I just want to whet your appetite by sketching out a few portraits of what the life of "letting go" might be like. Though the distinction may be artificial, we'll begin with individual choices and progress towards collective actions. In the final analysis, great personal dreams become common, and inspiring collective visions return to shape individual lives.

Before I outline a list of visionary activities, I want to make clear several principles that guide stewardship lifestyles. First, the point of this whole exercise of relinquishment and solidarity is empowerment of the dispossessed and not the enhancement of our own status or virtue. Stewardship is not charity—that's been its debilitating image for far too long. We undertake the dance of stewardship for the sake of empowerment, so that all people will be free, live fully, enjoy the music of God's earth. There is nothing more harmful and distasteful than overbearing Christian charity that "knows what's best for the poor."

For this reason we are called to let go of any pretence of righteousness, right thinking, or right living. Our task is to share our financial, social, and political power with those who have none. This empowerment takes patience and great personal integrity. Don't begin if you're thinking about what you're going to get out of it!

Second, we must be prepared to risk. There are no really safe ways to "let go." If relinquishment and solidarity are more than a pious posture, then we will not be able to stay the same. We will have to venture out onto the thin ice of uncertainty, and that's frightening. Few people have travelled this way before, and in many instances, we will be breaking new ground. That's never easy, but in a possessing society where having is highly valued, relinquishment is particularly threatening. It may well be that we risk not only our own personal well-being but also the respect of some friends in the process.

Risk is not a stranger to Christian discipleship. Belief, when it is understood as a guiding, fundamental principle, has always entailed some divergence from the trusted and safe path. Just by proclaiming faith in God, we set ourselves apart. We risk isolation and embarrassment within the bored and cynical circles of North American sophistication.

As we travel farther down this road, the risks will become more evident and the need for community will increase. Solidarity, relinquishment, and expectancy are kept alive through community, through the sharing of burdens and triumphs. Without a supportive network of a family or communal organization, the stewardly discipleship is onerous. Indeed, it is impossible for all but the most robust and self-determined souls.

Now to the vision! What follows is a list of projects and ideas for action that hint at the new world that awaits us. It is a world that is possible through solidarity and relinquishment.

1. To let go you have to know what you have. Draw up a list of your financial, social, intellectual, and political assets. Now ask yourself which of these "things" have you not really used, things which are no longer important or useful. Who could use these items? Is there some way in which the less important objects you possess could be used for the empowerment of the dispossessed? The simple act of knowing how much we have is a great step.

   Now, draw up a second list of what might be relinquished, and share this list with a friend. What do they think? Sharing an inventory of our earthly goods may give us clarity concerning their real importance.

2. Gandhi once said that he made many of his most difficult decisions through the recollection of the poorest person he

knew. What does my decision have to do with that impoverished one? Will it in any way influence his or her state? If so, how? Try using that line of reasoning when making important decisions during the next week or month. Share your logic with family members, and at the end of a designated period of time, ask how your life has changed.

3. Begin an analysis of the world from the standpoint of what you possess. It will take some digging for information, so begin with something in your house which is simple and well defined and ask how your possession of such an object influences the lives of the dispossessed. Look at a cup of coffee, for example. How much did it cost to make? How did you make it? Where did the coffee come from? How much was the person who owned the coffee plantation paid? What were the wages of the person who picked the beans? Who benefits from the current trading practices with respect to coffee? Who controls the price of coffee beans? How much coffee do you drink? Is there some other way to buy coffee aside from the regular brands at the local store that would help the growers and pickers directly?

Now that you've looked at coffee or some other domestic product, you will have the tools to examine other products and systems more precisely. In all this analysis, ask how your possession influences the poor and the marginalized.

Note: Can you imagine how our lives would change if we undertook these steps with seriousness? At the very least we would come to know who we are, what we have, how we decide on what we possess and how our lifestyle influences others. Wouldn't we begin to change, to adapt our dance to suit the music built into the created order itself?

4. Try "letting go" in certain small ways in your personal life. How about a partial fast? Fasting has a respected tradition within the Christian community. For a month, commit your-

self to foregoing lunch. Ask how it feels to be without. Why not join with others? Use your empty growling stomach to explore the nature of poverty. Why not take the time and extra money you've saved and use them with the dispossessed? If you fast as a group, look at what the Bible says about fasting and food (for example, Mark 2:18ff).

5. You must now take a step and put yourself in among the dispossessed. Let them teach you about their world. See yourself through their eyes.

This is not an easy step and not one I recommend lightly. It can very quickly lead to intrusive or unwanted interventions. Nevertheless, in the end, we who are powerful must begin to try to understand the experience of those who are marginalized by our wealthy North American world. I was once taught by a professor who expounded many radical visions of the way the world should be transformed. Fortunately he was married to a woman who set about doing just that. At one point it was humorously suggested that she put her feet where his mouth was. Well, the time has come for us, for the church, and for powerful white males to do the same. We must put our bodies in the place of those who have been forgotten.

How do you take this step with sensitivity and authenticity? Each will find their own path, but I believe one place to begin is with knowledge. Just try to understand one dimension of the crisis. Seriously try to understand it. The natural process will draw you deeper and deeper into the subject matter until you find yourself in a different company, a different neighbourhood, a different house.

Here's an example. If you want to stand in solidarity with people living on a fixed income, where do you begin? How about the local welfare office? Why not call the director and ask for an interview? Then you could search about for the advocates of those living on income assistance. There are self-help groups in most major urban centres. What do they say about their plight?

155

Then there are books and magazines, television, and radio. Ask yourself what the dominant image of people on welfare is. Does the media's portrayal agree with what you've heard?

Now ask how your local church works with these folk. Where do they sit? Are they in the pews on Sunday morning or outside the pastor's office on weekdays? Maybe it's both. Where are the marginalized in our congregations? Do they come in to our programmes? Why not? Should they get involved in this church? Should the church get involved in their struggles?

Can you see how a church gets involved? It begins with simple inquiries and very soon moves to talking with the victims of our possessing world and walking their path with them. We can travel down this road for some time without risk or change, but eventually we are faced with a choice. I wish it were otherwise, but resources are limited and human energy is a finite commodity. There will come a time when we have to choose. With whom do we work? Where will we expend our energy? Who needs us most?

Can you imagine what our church, our families would be like if we made a choice, a clear decision to side with the marginalized? What would be possible if we harnessed the financial and social resources of the believing community?

Note: There is something we must remind ourselves of at this point. Poverty is a political choice. It is not a necessary dimension of human existence. All too often Jesus is quoted out of context: "the poor will be with you always" (Matt. 26:10). It is implied that poverty is a intrinsic part of God's creation. It isn't. Poverty is a political choice. Oppression, abuse, destitution are all tolerated by our society as regrettable, but acceptable, costs in maintaining our present economic order. As a people we decide to tolerate a certain level of poverty when we choose an economic system that concentrates financial power in the hands of a few.

Is it possible that a people would choose not to have poverty, would choose instead to eradicate destitution? In some countries

*they have done just that. I live in the hope that others will do the
same.*

6. Assuming we sense the need to stand in solidarity with the
    homeless and the dispossessed that we meet and assuming
    that we are in search of a more authentic lifestyle, the sky is
    the limit for what we might envision.

    What about a community of planned relinquishment? Over
    the next five years, your family and your church will let go of
    some of its precious commodities for the sake of responding
    to the struggles of the dispossessed. For the first year, you
    relinquish the electrical appliances you own and transfer the
    savings on the utility bill to a self-help group. Or as a church,
    you might give up church bulletins and advertising, giving
    the surplus to the M&S fund. That money could be used to
    send food to the Horn of Africa. In the second year, you
    might give up some of your space and use it for those who
    have no place to meet, no home. Or you might give up using
    banking institutions that protect church trust funds. Instead
    of putting your money into blue chip stocks and government
    bonds, why not invest it in more ethically appropriate fash-
    ions, such as housing co-operatives, ecological ventures,
    worker co-operatives? They all need capital. Why not give
    them yours? How about the several church funds that sup-
    port local extension work or inner-city missions?

    Can you imagine how the world might be changed if even
    a few of the thousands of churches began to invest their
    financial reserves in an alternative manner?

    In the third year, you could relinquish your vacation time
    as individuals to build houses for the homeless. As a church,
    you might give up paid ministerial staff and use the funds for
    alternative outreach work. So the years pass. What a renewed
    people we could become!

7. This is a project for someone wanting to relinquish power.
    Why not add up the total financial assets held in trust by the

local churches of one town or city? What do these funds represent in terms of real political power? How could this power be used to empower the poor? In my case, I can throw a rock from the front door of the church where I work and hit a number of other church buildings. In that small area, I know our combined trust funds would easily exceed one million dollars. What could we do with that money if we found the courage to let go?

I am aware of the sobering advice of church trustees who point out that these monies are used to preserve the church for future generations, but a stronger voice calls me. In the difficult times of the depression, there were churches that mortgaged their buildings to help out the starving and desperate farmers on the prairies. That was a great risk they took. Are times less difficult now? Doesn't the world need our money more than ever? Can't we risk the future generation's church for the sake of today's need?

8. What would happen to your family if you declared your home to be a safe place and made a concerted effort to open your doors to all those who needed sanctuary? Would your home be different in any way? Would you view ownership differently? What would happen if we declared that our churches were sanctuaries, specific locations for those who sought safety? This is not a new vision. Monasteries and catacombs served the purpose of harbouring the lost and protecting the victimized. Why not re-establish this traditional vision as the guiding light for the North American church?

There are several churches in Cuba that have converted their Christian education wings into dormitories, places of comfort and rest for travellers. Could we not do the same for the homeless, for battered women, abused children, for panhandlers? How would we exercise our stewardship differently if our church became a sanctuary for those whom society rejects: the welfare recipient, gays and lesbians, the unemployed?

9. Have you ever imagined your church as the leader in establishing co-operative consumerism? Religious communities have fostered work co-operatives and housing co-operatives. Why not a buyers co-operative? This could be as simple as the co-operative purchase of bulk food items, but I envision something more far reaching. Could we not establish models for joint ownership of land, cars, houses, cottages? As a church, we have been quite skilful in the creation of stewardship models for the sharing of financial resources. What about similar programmes for sharing our real property? Why not turn the church into an alternative community where, as was the case with the first Christian gatherings, "all things are held in common"? What structures could we create to counteract the ill effects of consumerism? How about church-sponsored land trusts, co-operative housing, job sharing? The list is endless.

Note: This vision of an alternative community will not be easy to establish. Many folk will call it impractical or utopian. I prefer to see it as the prophetically imaginative spirit at work. Whatever its label, there is no doubt that some of the powerful members of our society will find such "church" activities uncomfortable or disturbing.

10. Could our church communities become havens of credit relief? I once suggested to a church that was situated across the street from a large shopping mall that their role in the community might be to discourage inappropriate credit. Open a booth in a shopping mall with a sign that says, "Don't do it!", and establish a financial counselling service to help people break the consumer's addiction to credit. What a service and a witness this could be!

Conclusion and Questions for Debate

I love to dream. The possibilities for service are awe inspiring and the list of ideas could go on endlessly. The chief concern is contextuality. Make sure you establish your own unique vision, one that speaks to you and your local church and allows the wider mission of Christ to progress in your setting.

All I have offered here are rough sketches of a vision. I encourage you to take one of the above ten ideas, or one of your own imagining, form a group, and explore what it might mean for you and your community of faith if you took that vision seriously. Just keep saying, "What if..."

Conclusion

The band and the crowd went off like a bomb. People were danc-
ing all through the tables to the back of the room and behind the
bar. People were dancing in the rest rooms and around the pool
tables. Dancing for themselves, for the Indian, for God and
Mammon. Dancing in the face of hospital rooms, mortuaries,
funeral services and cemeteries. And for a while nobody died.

—Fulghum 1986, 125

I have explored relinquishment, solidarity, and expectancy as
the subject of three distinct workshops. However, as must be
obvious by now, they cannot be separated. They exist in a constant dialogue, intertwined in an exhilarating dance. No one
relinquishes forever and ever and no one acts in solidarity on a
consistent level. And how many people can hope without having
at least a few moments of despair?

There are times when we sit out the dance, choosing to find
peace or rest or escape. We are human, after all. No matter who
we are or where we have travelled, God calls us back into the
dance. God reaches out and pulls us into the cycle of solidarity
that elicits relinquishment and fosters hope.

It's a circular affair, this dance of stewardship. Each time we
come back to the beginning, we discover there is more to learn.
The music of life changes, and so does the dance. Each day we
are all invited back onto the floor, to correct yesterday's steps

and pick up today's rhythm and anticipate tomorrow's beat.

The image of a dancing steward may seem rather flippant and light. After all, stewardship and discipleship, like most things religious, are heavy and staid. They are sombre and sobering work. How many sermons have told us so? Faith is no laughing matter!

Perhaps that is what I personally must relinquish first: the assumption that faith is supposed to be a bit dull, always sacrosanct, and that a serious examination of stewardly discipleship must be grinding and uninteresting. Perhaps I must let go of my restraint and risk being a fool, a failure for Christ's sake.

When I can free myself from this false sense of discipleship, when I can feel the winds of God's Spirit stirring a greater vision within me, then I want to shout and sing, run and dance. Yes, I want to dance. So in conclusion, what more can I say except, "Let's dance! Come, join again in a journey of discipleship, in the journey of the cross!"

In making that invitation, I am well aware that we do not join in this special dance on our own merit or because we're particularly virtuous or talented. It's not our worthiness that makes us dancing stewards; rather, we're asked to dance in spite of our unworthiness. Who cares about the clumsy steps? Join in anyway. Stewardship lifestyles are on-the-job training.

In this respect, we could say that the life of solidarity, relinquishment, and hope is God's gift. No one is an "expert" or more prepared than anyone else. To relinquish in response to the call to solidarity is an act of grace. We don't gain any heavenly merit; it's not something we can do of our own accord. Letting go is also sheer gift. And to hope with great passion, to have a vision of what we might become on this journey of the cross, that also is not our doing. That too is God's gift.

Apart from the gracefulness of the invitation to this dance of stewardly lifestyles, the time to dance is now. When the hand is held out for the dance, the moment to accept is now. There may be no other time or place, no other dance, no other motivation.

If we respond, the dance will probably begin in small ways. It may not even look like a dance at first. There may be no band, no hall, but it does begin now, in the new life we seek. In our own communities, in the church where we worship, in our living rooms, in our classrooms, offices, or playgrounds. Wherever you are reading this book, the dance begins here and now. Look around!

Living in an affluent world that desires immediate gratification, we might be tempted to view the "real" mission of stewardship as taking place in locations with more "needy" people, such as El Salvador or Somalia, in the black ghetto or on a Native reserve. Don't believe it! The dance starts here with our own backyard decisions. What we decide in affluent North America has significance, great significance for other nations and peoples.

There is a surprising and frightening immediacy implicit within the gospel's challenge to build stewardship lifestyles. Jesus did not wait or postpone the call: "Follow me"; "Take up your cross." The time to undertake the dance is now; the place to do it is here where we live.

There is one last story to be told, one which speaks of the challenge, cost, and excitement of the dance that awaits us.

When the Canadian west was invaded by white settlers, many denominations adopted a practice of sending their missionaries to newly established towns. At regular intervals along the rail line, water towers were constructed, and the towns that grew up at these junctures eventually had need of a minister.

Church organizations would send out eager pastors by train to organize the local residents of frontier settlements into communities of faith. As is the case with many human endeavours, a competition arose among churches. Who could serve the greatest number of little towns? Which church was growing the fastest? In the Canadian west, the competition was between the Methodists and Presbyterians. Clergy went off in a mad dash in order to arrive first at a specific town and turn the unsuspecting folk into either good Methodists or good Presbyterians.

On one particular day, two ministers were dispatched to the same village on a spur line in Saskatchewan. By chance (or divine providence, depending on your view), they both boarded the same train and sat in the same car. Each knew the other's destination, as secrets were loosely kept in the rough and tumble of outpost settlements. They eyed each other with suspicion.

The Methodist became agitated as he pondered his ill fortune and wondered how he could get off the train first and run around and claim the town for the Wesleyan tradition before this lowly Presbyterian could interfere: "Surely John Wesley would have known what to do."

The Presbyterian, being more of a realist, decided that there was not much hope of capturing this town for the true faith. So he sat reflecting on the dilemma of predestination with the air of a disinterested Calvinist (a contradiction in terms, I admit).

Presently, the Methodist got up and walked to the front of the car. John Wesley had answered his prayers. The undaunted pastor knew what had to be done. He had resolved to ride the entire trip on the step of the train car, knowing that when the train slowed down at the platform, he would be the first person to alight onto the platform of that, as yet, pagan village. He would immediately say a Methodist prayer, albeit rather briefly, declare the town for the only true faith, and then turn around in time to greet his brother in Christ, welcoming him to a "good" Methodist town.

Satisfied with his plan, he bobbed up and down over the prairie, dreaming about his first sermon in a newly built white chapel at the crossroads of the fast-approaching settlement. He relished a vision of the wild revival that would ensue just after the first homily ended.

At one point, the hapless Presbyterian minister passed by on his way forward to the dining car. "Typical of so many Presbyterians," thought the Methodist. "In the heat of battle, when worlds are won and lost, they're off to eat." Chuckling to himself, he went back to the great revival in his mind.

Once the town was in sight, and the train began to slow down, the Methodist prepared for his leap of faith. The brakes screeched and steam engulfed the platform as the pastor jumped with all the determination of an Olympic athlete. He landed upright and was immediately and warmly embraced in the arms of the Presbyterian minister, who welcomed him to a "fine" Presbyterian village.

The Presbyterian had not gone to lunch. Rather, he had gone to sit on the cow-catcher of the train and had jumped off before the rest of the cars had reached the town!

The denomination does not matter. The vision of a Christian sitting on the cow-catcher, while it may appear comical or even absurd, captures the hope-filled lifestyle of a Christian steward. Here is one who has left the comforts behind, relinquished his place, and sat at the edge of risk. Here is one who lives where the sparks are flying, the wind is hurtling around, and the suffering is great. But the vision, the vision is breath taking. Here is a dancing steward!

Annotated Bibliography

Avila, Charles. 1983. *Ownership: Early Christian Teaching*. Maryknoll: Orbis. A helpful guide to early Christian pronouncements on private property and the idea of ownership.

Bassler, Jouette M. 1991. *God and Mammon*. Nashville: Abingdon. An excellent, very accessible examination of the ways in which people ask for money in the Christian scriptures. It includes a discussion of Paul's great collection and the means by which the first disciples funded their missionary endeavours.

Bonhoeffer, Dietrich. 1937. *The Cost of Discipleship*. London: SCM Press. A classic text that explores the costs involved in faithful discipleship. It contains the central idea of "costly grace," which I have in mind when I speak of "real hope" and "the grace which grabs" us as believers. Bonhoeffer eventually paid the price for his outspoken theology when he was executed by the Nazis in 1945.

_____. 1953. *Letters and Papers from Prison*. Trans. R. Fuller, Bethge, E., ed. London: SCM Press. A foundational text for rethinking the religious exercise in the modern era.

Brueggemann, Walter. 1978. *The Prophetic Imagination*. Philadelphia: Fortress Press. A volume that has done more to assist pastors in their wish to live and preach prophetically than any other text I know. He writes: "The task of prophetic ministry is to nurture, nourish and evoke a consciousness and perception of the dominant culture around us." It's very readable and rich in insights.

Czerny, Michael, and Jamie Swift. 1984. *Getting Started on Social Analysis in Canada*. Toronto: Between the Lines. I have used this text in many courses on social analysis. It begins with simple ideas and builds into a complex examination of the interrelationships between poverty and powerlessness. While it begins from a Canadian point of view, its insights are easily transferable to other industrialized nations.

Duchrow, Ulrich. 1987. *Global Economy*. Geneva: WCC Publications. This text addresses the rich churches of the West, especially the churches of Germany. The author attempts to identify possible ways in which Christians can establish a new economic order and live their covenant relationship with God in responsible ways.

Ellul, Jacques. 1964. *The Technological Society*. New York: Vintage Books. Now recognized as a very important text, Ellul here offers an excellent and far-reaching analysis of the motive powers behind the technological revolution of the modern era.

Endo, Shusaku. 1976. *Silence*. New York: Taplinger Publishing Co. Trans. William Johnston. A novel valuable for its insight into Christology.

Fulghum, Robert. 1986. *All I Really Need to Know I Learned in Kindergarten*. New York: Ivy Books. Fulghum's work is now well known. While he has written several other collections of stories, I still enjoy this work most. It offers a depth of understanding of human existence combined with a delightful and healthy playfulness. His stories do lead us in the right direction: away from conspicuous self-centredness.

Goodger, W. D., ed. 1981. *Spotlighting Stewardship*. Toronto: United Church Publishing House. A good text containing many key articles that shaped the path of stewardship studies.

Gutierrez, Gustavo. 1989. *On Job: God Talk and the Problem of the Suffering of the Innocent*. Maryknoll: Orbis Books. A very refreshing examination of an ancient question. Gutierrez re-establishes a new image of God, a God who loves with great abandon.

Hall, Douglas John. 1976. *Lighten our Darkness*. Philadelphia: Westminster Press. This may possibly be Hall's best work. This text outlines his theology of the cross as an indigenous theology for the North American context. While I don't refer to it directly, much of Hall's thought is found in the sections of this book relating to Christ-centred solidarity.

_____. 1985. *The Stewardship of Life in the Kingdom of Death*. New York: Friendship Press. The particular tone of this text may be a bit dated since many people imagine the threat of nuclear destruction to be remote. We no longer see ourselves as living in a kingdom of death. The message is still valid as far as I can see.

_____. 1986. *Imaging God*. Grand Rapids, Mich.: Eerdmans. An excellent text for the re-examination of the Christian understanding of God.

_____. 1990. *The Steward*. Grand Rapids, Mich.: Eerdmans. Now recognized as *the* classic text on Christian stewardship, this book reads well and has many insights to offer. I have listed here the revised edition.

Hart, John. 1984. *The Spirit of the Earth*. New York: Paulist Press. A good text that examines the ecological and theological considerations of a Christian stewardship of creation.

Keen, Sam. 1991. *Fire in the Belly*. New York: Bantam Books. An excellent exploration of the journey men travel to find maturity. Keen is practical and prophetic at the same time, resulting in a tone that is comforting, yet disquieting.

McGill, Arthur. 1987. *Death and Life*. Philadelphia: Fortress Press. A small book, but full of insights into North American life. McGill's analysis is profound and much of my material on human neediness arises from his thought.

McNaught, Kenneth. 1959. *A Prophet in Politics*. Toronto: University of Toronto Press. The foundational biography of J. S. Woodsworth, founder of the C.C.F. Party in Canada and a central figure in the Social Gospel movement.

Moltmann, J. 1974. *The Crucified God*. London: SCM Press. Moltmann's book is now considered to be a central Christological text. It contains a good deal of material on the theology of the cross.

Morgan, Elizabeth, Van Weigel, and Eric Debaufe. 1989. *Global Poverty and Personal Responsibility*. New York: Paulist Press. I found this to be most helpful in trying to understanding our role in global economic justice. Morgan leaves us with a feeling of expectation and hope rather than guilt. A very helpful text for study groups.

Murphy, Nordan, ed. 1985. *Teaching and Preaching Stewardship*. New York: NCCC. An excellent collection of articles that still have merit in the present dialogue concerning the place of stewardship in Christian discipleship.

Reumann, John. 1992. *Stewardship and the Economy of God*. Grand Rapids, Mich.: Eerdmans. Reumann illustrates how the modern use of the term "stewardship" is actually derived from the biblical record. His analysis of its roots is quite informative.

Roop, Eugene. 1992. *Let the Rivers Run*. Grand Rapids, Mich.: Eerdmans. A study of the Hebrew scriptures and their understanding of the idea of stewardship. Very good reading.

Saiving, Valorie. 1979. The Human Situation: A Feminist View. *Womanspirit Rising*. Carol Christ, Judith Plaskow, eds. New York: Harper & Row. A very insightful article on the difference between male and female conditioning and the influences of this conditioning on Christian anthropology.

Shumacher, E. F. 1973. *Small is Beautiful*. San Francisco: Harper & Row. This book has been a classic since its first printing. It calls the consumptive Western world to account for the principles of "bigness" and "efficiency." Schumacher offers a model for moving into the future that is workable and ecologically desirable.

Scott, R. B. Y., and Gregory Vlastos, eds. 1989. *Towards the Christian Revolution*. Kingston: Ronald P. Frye & Co. Though it was first written in the 1930s, this is still an excellent book for those who seek to understand the Social Gospel message.

Sider, Ronald J. 1977. *Rich Christians in an Age of Hunger*. New York: Paulist Press. This is the most widely regarded text on Christian responsibility in the modern world. Sider concentrates on the issue of hunger, but his insights are applicable to the wider issues of poverty and oppression.

Vallet, Ron. 1989. *Stepping Stones of the Steward*. Grand Rapids, Mich.: Eerdmans. An excellent text containing many stories and illustrations that show how the Gospels develop the idea of Christian stewardship.

Wallis, Jim. 1984. *Agenda for a Biblical People: A New Edition*. San Francisco: Harper & Row. An excellent study of what it means to be a faithful disciple in our modern society.

_____. 1987. *The Rise of Christian Conscience.* San Francisco: Harper & Row. Wallis is down to earth and concrete. His experiences in the Sojourner's community in Washington, D.C., ensure that his call to a new conscience is compelling and clear.

_____. 1990. The Second Reformation Has Begun. *Sojourners* 10 (January). An article with many good, real-life stories of the plight of the poor and the new awakening among Christian churches as a result of the confrontation with poverty.

Weber, Max. 1958. *The Protestant Ethic and Spirit of Capitalism.* New York: Charles Scribner's Sons. A foundational text on the interplay between capitalist ideas and Christian theology.

Wiesel, Elie. 1969. *Night.* New York: Discus Books. From his experiences in the concentration camps of World War II, Wiesel writes a very powerful novel touching on the themes of despair and hope, justice and injustice, day and night in the human soul.